ROCK GUITAR BIBLE

DISCOVER THE SECRETS OF CLASSIC ROCK,
LEARN LICKS IN THE STYLE OF ROCK LEGENDS AND
CREATE DISTORTED-EXPLOSIVE ROCK MUSIC OF YOUR OWN

GUITAR HEAD

✉ gh@theguitarhead.com ☐ ☐ /theguitarhead

Disclaimer

Dedication

---

*We dedicate this book to the complete
Guitar Head team,
supporters, well-wishers and
the Guitar Head community.*

*It goes without saying that we
would not have gotten
this far without
your encouragement,
critique and support*

Table of Contents

Free Guitar Head Bonuses

Audio Files

All Guitar Head books come with audio tracks for the licks inside the book. These audio tracks are an integral part of the book - they ensure you are playing the charts and chords the way they are intended to be played.

Lifetime Access To Guitar Head Community

Being around like-minded people is the first step to being successful at anything. The Guitar Head community is a place where you can find people who are willing to listen to your music, answer your questions or talk anything guitar.

Email Newsletters Sent Directly To Your Inbox

We send regular guitar lessons and tips to all our subscribers. Our subscribers are also the first to know about Guitar Head giveaways and holiday discounts.

Free PDF

Guitar mastery is all about the details! Getting the small things right and avoiding mistakes that can slow your guitar journey by years. So, we wrote a book about 25 of the most common mistakes guitarists make and decided to give it for free to all Guitar Head readers.

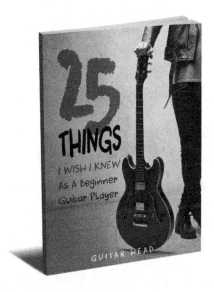

You can grab a copy of the free book, the audio files and subscribe to the newsletter by following the link below.

All these bonuses are a 100% free, with no strings attached. You won't need to enter any personal details other than your first name and email address.

To get your bonuses, go to: ***www.theguitarhead.com/bonus***

Book Profile

Difficulty Level: Intermediate

Technical knowledge you need before reading this book:

The book is designed to teach you classic rock in complete and unlock your creative mind to write powerful rock riffs and licks of your own. However, to stay true to the concept of classic rock, I will not be discussing the basics of guitar playing.

So, I recommend the following skills before getting into the book:

- » Basics of guitar- Tuning, how to hold, and finger independence
- » Chord shifting and ability to play chord progression.
- » Fretboard visualisation
- » Basics of rhythm- Note values and right hand strumming
- » Knowledge of scales and keys

Suggested reading before this book:

If you want to understand the fretboard, you can check out our *"Guitar Fretboard"* book before starting the classic rock.

How To Use This Book

On our way to rock and roll, we're going to establish some rules but feel free to break them all. We're here to rock and the spirit of this wild music is present in every word.

So, read carefully and apply at will.

A rocking world is waiting for you starting in chapter one.

Do The Exercises And Grasp The Concept Musically

This book is not just a guide of steps or a list of important concepts you should apply to be a rocking guitarist. We want to take our teachings several steps forward, and for that, we're giving you useful, stage-ready, road-tested licks, tricks, and tips.

Yes, this book goes far beyond your usual "googling of information."

In the following pages, you'll find not only the reason why every foundational brick has its place in the kingdom of rock and roll but also how to build your rocking chops from scratch.

I hope you're ready because we're going to go deep into every topic as we help you become a better guitar player in every single lesson.

This book is a practical guide to becoming a better rock and roll guitar player, period.

Make It Yours, Experiment, And Have Fun

We want you to copy us, to steal from us, to play our exercises as much as you need to make them part of your playing. Once our licks cross that border, they become yours, carry your unique playing style, and help you grow your catalog as a guitar player.

Also, from a songwriting point of view, we'll go deep into the mechanics of hit-making with a plethora of examples that cover all styles and emotions. We'll unlock the door to inspiration with information. Furthermore, there's space to document your first-ever finished song too.

This first glimpse at the creation process could turn out to be the beginning of an amazing career as a player, a writer, and a performer.

Yet, if it doesn't, if you play the guitar for the pure joy that it means to relate with the instrument, I hope these pages help you learn more about your idols and play closer to what you always wanted.

This is a book that encourages you to play a lot; it is a book to read with the guitar in your hands.

So, read it and play it as much as you need to make it your own, but above all, have fun with it.

Do it the Rock and Roll way.

Forget About Chapter Order, Find Your Path

This book is a big lesson on rock and roll that starts from absolute scratch; we're ground zero of your revolution.

Yet, if you feel like you already know what you're reading when you start from the beginning, you can either revisit the information and have some fun with known stuff or flip toward the part of the book that interests you the most.

For example, if you're more interested in learning how to create epic solos than songwriting because you're the lead guitar player of the band and the singer takes care of the composing, you might go straight to scales, licks, and riffs.

Yet, this book also works holistically because the more you know about songwriting, the better you'll be at soloing. Yes, that is something that this book does a lot: it shows you the invisible links between the song and the solo that became the secret of so many guitar gods in rock history.

Feel free to choose your path and follow your curiosity; who knows, maybe you find a new spin on a known topic.

Every Chapter Is Revision Material

Speaking about your path in acquiring the avalanche of information in this book (really, the material awaiting you a few pages away is overwhelming) we recommend that you go back often to revise information.

By going back, what we mean is that, beyond getting the lick from the exercise and playing it perfectly, you can go back a second time and try to learn the feel of the lick; the little nuances that make it unique.

Then, go back a third time and try working out the mechanics of the lick. Why is it a good or bad-sounding lick? Why does it work? What is the scale; what can you build around it? How can you make it better?

Every chapter in this book contains more questions and answers than you might spot on a first read.

So, go back to the chapters and make the information here the solid foundations of your guitar wisdom.

Plus, you might find a couple of anecdotes that put a smile on your face or take some weight off your shoulders.

Learn every lesson down to its very mechanics and make the most out of this book.

This Is Not A Book To Finish, It Is A One-Way Ticket To Playing Better

Some books, many books, require you to read them from beginning to end. That way, you can grasp the plot and the characters, and watch the story unravel and resolve.

This book is not like that; you can think of this book as a manual. Yes, this is a practical manual to becoming an all-around better rock and roll guitar player.

You can also think of it as a handbook you reach for whenever you want and revise any concept.

Furthermore, this book can also become a source of inspiration. We poured our heart, soul, and experience into every page. Hopefully, all of that will reach you and inspire you to keep making amazing rock music.

So, if you don't finish this book, don't worry. Who knows? Maybe you'll stop playing in that band behind the composing singer and want to form a project of your own. Suddenly, you remember this book and we can help you make your first complete song and learn what happens behind the curtain for songwriters.

So, if you don't finish this book right now, don't worry. We can help you in every step you make toward becoming a better rock and roll guitar player.

Make The Most Out Of Bonus Track

This book contains a lot of guitar playing that was specially designed and thought to help you grasp some concepts better and teach you the nuances of our instrument.

These lessons will come in the shape of notation and tabs so you can follow not only the tempo and the notes, but also the moves, like bendings, vibratos, and more.

We know that for some players that approach is enough but we want to help as many fellow rockers as we can. Therefore, we took the lessons one step further and created an audio example of each.

We strongly believe that you'll be able to hear and copy the exact dynamics and details that each exercise proposes once you hear it played by one of the experts in the office.

So, let bonus track be the lighthouse to sail the stormy ocean of rock and roll always in the right direction.

Your one-way golden ticket to being a better rock and roll guitar player, some very useful tips, a lot of playing, and obnoxious amounts of fun begin just a little further.

Buckle up, grab your favorite guitar, and get ready for the ride of your life.

The History of Rock n' Roll

> " That Rock n' Roll, uh? That rock n' roll just won't go away. It might hibernate from time to time, sink back into the swamp. But is always waiting there just around the corner ready to make its way back through the sludge and smash through the glass ceiling looking better than ever. Yeah, that rock n' roll, it seems as if it's fading away sometimes, but it will never die. And there's nothing you can do about it. "

These are the words of modern rock n' roll genius, Alex Turner, as he and his band, Arctic Monkeys, received the Album of the Year award in 2014.

30 seconds later, he smashed the microphone on the fancy floor of the fancy ceremony.

With those simple words and a bold act of rebellion, he managed to summarize the very spirit of rock n' roll. Yes, it's a style that has mutated infinitely in the past 70 years but refuses to go away.

Rock n' roll will never die.

Yet, we are here to understand where it all began. So, buckle up because this time machine is ready to take you to the epicenter of one of the biggest musical and cultural revolutions humankind has lived through so far.

It's time to get the mojo going, to get groovy, and, above all, to get rocking.

Go, find your favorite leather jacket and comb that hair slick back because here we go.

How Did It All Begin?

To understand the birth of rock and roll, we must first understand the nature of the people who created it. Yes, rock and roll didn't come down from a starship traveling millions of light years; it was created by people like you and me.

But what was the particular landscape that allowed rock and roll to be born?

Well, to begin with, it comes from a very particular country that was home to immigration from a plethora of influences. Yes, we're talking about the USA, a country where rhythm and blues, country music, bluegrass, folk, boogie-woogie, soul, gospel, jazz, and swing music coexisted in a very nurtured and particular music scene.

Moreover, people from every walk of life created and shared this music in all kinds of venues from churches to bars.

You have to think we're talking about the 1930s and 1940s; record players weren't a common home appliance until the sixties. So, options were the radio or live musicians to hear any melodies at all.

Furthermore, after WWII, the world was in a shortage of fuel and in a delicate financial state. Therefore, the big jazz bands became too costly for bars and were replaced by simpler, smaller combos featuring drums, bass, guitar, and little else.

Parallel to that, a plethora of amplified electric musical instruments made their way into shops across the United States. The first electric guitars, basses, and their amplifiers became available to make musicians sound louder.

Also, the appearance of the drum kit and its transformation into a musical standard widely across the country for venue stages was decisive for the rhythm section.

Finally, the black population moved to big urban places such as New York, Cleveland, St. Louis, Chicago, Memphis, Detroit, and Buffalo. This generated a very odd phenomenon that was black and white people living closer than ever in history.

Thus, styles such as waltzes, polkas, folk, bluegrass, and Dixieland Jazz, were mixed with gospel, blues, and swing; styles that were popularized by and popular among the African-American population.

What came out of this interesting clash?

Well, we can think of the appearance of styles such as rhythm and blues, perhaps, the closest precursor of rock n roll we can find together with the not-so-famous jump blues.

These Are Rock N' Roll's Biggest Influences

Rock and roll is the outcome of a very interesting social phenomenon that happened during a very particular time on Earth.

Let me take you back to 1940, the year *Billboard* was created. Back then, the music was divided into three categories and then charted: Pop, country and western, and rhythm and blues.

Believe it or not, back in the early '40s, one of the main drivers of these charts was jukeboxes; because that was one of the few ways people could listen to music. Moreover, there were half a million jukeboxes in the USA in 1940.

So, the ranking was made utilizing the information from jukeboxes, record sales, and disc jockeys playing it on the radio. By the way, in 1950, 96% of the homes in the USA had a radio.

Speaking from a commercial point of view, we can say that the "Rhythm and Blues" column was dedicated to the African-American population while country and western was reserved for white people.

But why is this important, you might be wondering?

Well, because it shows exactly where rock and roll's influences come from. On one hand, you have the country and western music that most of the white audience was listening to. On the other hand, you have rhythm and blues, a style of music made mostly by and aimed at an African-American audience.

What happened was that these columns started mixing with each other rapidly, and, suddenly, white teenagers and youngsters started buying rhythm and blues records. They couldn't help but be moved by the hip sound and the uplifting, dance-ready beat.

Moreover, the simple melodies and loud lyrics (derived largely from gospel) were radio-ready and aimed to make people shout them loud as they danced.

On the other side, the traditional elements of western and country music became more palpable in a mix of styles that was appealing to all youth regardless of skin color or social status.

So, classic, groundbreaking artists such as Chuck Berry, Little Richard, Fats Domino, Howlin' Wolf, Sister Rosetta Tharpe, Ike Turner, and Arthur Crudup were joined by other artists like Elvis Presley, Johnny Cash, Carl

Rock Guitar Bible

Perkins, Jerry Lee Lewis, and Roy Orbison who brought a new element to the mix: country music.

A new rhythm that was to outdo all of them emerged from this mixture, and the world was forever changed. That rhythm is rock and roll and it took over the world really fast; as a revolution should.

When Was The First Rock N' Roll Played?

Although a lot has been written and said about which the first rock and roll record of all time was, it is safe to say that rock and roll didn't emerge overnight, but it is the outcome of a musical (r)evolution.

Therefore, we can think of records that date back to the mid-1940s like Sister Rosetta Tharpe's "Strange Things Happening Every Day" (1944) or Arthur Crudup's "That's All Right" (1946) or "Move it on Over" by Hank Williams (1947).

But were these the breakthrough records? Well, it was a process that slowly shaped the ear and musical taste of a generation. All these records named above were seeds planted in the ears of rock and roll's future audience.

In this sense, it is important to talk about a man in particular named Sam Phillips. He was the founder and owner of Sun Records, which was one of the very few (if not the only) studios that took chances with walk-in artists.

One of those walk-in geniuses was a young 18-year-old boy called Elvis Presley. He recorded two songs for his mum in 1953 and was called again by Phillips one year later to play with two white musicians the now-legendary guitarist Scotty Moore and Bill Black, who played standup bass.

Elvis ended up singing "That's All Right" (Arthur Crudup's hit from 1946) instead of ballads. It was a crossover from an early, African-American

20

pioneer transformed by the voice of one of the biggest rock and roll singers of all time.

That was a historical moment because, although it wasn't the first time a white singer covered a rhythm and blues song, it was the first time an artist from a different genre emerged, a crossover artist that appealed to all 3 columns of the *Billboard* publication.

The song had African-American roots in the rhythm but was clearly marked by Elvis' country upbringing.

Phillips gave it to a rhythm and blues DJ and it was an overnight sensation.

But beyond Elvis, Sam Phillips also produced artists like B. B. King, Ike Turner, Howlin' Wolf, Carl Perkins, Jerry Lee Lewis, Johnny Cash, and Roy Orbison. Together with them, he produced all-time classics like "Blue Suede Shoes" "Mystery Train" "Folsom Prison Blues" "I Walk the Line" "Whole Lotta Shakin' Going On" "Great Balls of Fire" and the list goes on.

So, it is safe to say that the road that took rock and roll to the radios, jukeboxes, and record stores in the USA during the early fifties (and continued to do so for 70+ years after) came from the mid-'40s rhythm and blues, country, and pop artists.

Where Was Rock N' Roll Born?

Although there is much skepticism about where rock and roll originated, most historians and experts in the matter agree that the first radio station to play "Rock and Roll" music under that name was in Cleveland, Ohio.

The year was 1951, and the program (from 11.15PM to 2AM) was called "The Moondog Rock & Roll House Party" and it was hosted and musicalized by Alan Freed. Together with Leo Mintz, the owner of Record Rendezvous, they started playing Rhythm and Blues records for the entire nation calling it "Rock& Roll".

Furthermore, Freed will very often shout "Rock & Roll" to the audience creating a sudden wave of attention and fanatics. The wild, irreverent style of rock and roll started to take shape beyond just the music.

Soon after, Freed wanted to be crowned as the king of the *Moondoggers*, who was his loyal audience. So, he created the first-ever rock and roll show under the name of "Moondog Coronation Ball". The year was 1952, and the event was to take place at the Cleveland Arena.

That night, the show lasted only one song because nobody was ready for the overwhelming crowd that showed up to the event. It took the police and the fire department to evacuate the building.

The following day, every newspaper in the area, and then the nation, was covering the story of why rock and roll and its evil impulses should be ended.

Isn't this a very rock and roll thing to happen?

Wasn't the style born from the irreverence of youngsters looking for a reason to howl at the moon and dance until their feet hurt?

Moreover, isn't that same spirit the one that still fuels rock shows today?

Well, if you think that the answer to that question is yes, then we can agree that the name, the myth, and the legend were born in Cleveland, Ohio.

That being said, the music that started in the mid-'40s came from large urban spaces occupied by the African-American population.

The First Wave Of Rock N' Roll, Meet The Pioneers

There are several figures in what can be called the "first wave" of rock and roll. We're going to go through some of the most important ones of this early generation.

The generation we're talking about is the one that rocked the world between 1955 and 1959; before the almighty '60s and '70s took rock and roll to the epic instances they did.

Before all that, rock and roll was very simply the hip music of the moment, the one that teenagers and youngsters wanted to hear and dance to; it was all about having fun and breaking the rules.

Chuck Berry

The person who came closer to putting all the pieces that make what we now know as rock and roll together was no other than the celebrated, late Chuck Berry.

He was a confessed country music fan, an avid rhythm and blues singer, and a non-traditional but absolute guitar virtuoso. He put together the rhythm section, simplified the melodies and lyrics, and turned the jump blues piano players two-note riffs into historic guitar licks creating a unique sound.

Thus, he was the first one to bring all elements of what we know today as rock and roll into the shape of songs for the first time.

He did that by breaking all the rules; AKA, the rock and roll way.

Bill Haley & His Comets

"Nine, ten, eleven o'clock, twelve o'clock, rock.

We're gonna rock around the clock tonight"

Do these lyrics sound familiar to you? Yes, they belong to the once biggest-selling single in rock and roll history: "Rock around the clock" by Bill Haley & His Comets from 1954.

But that's not all, what about the line "Shake, rattle, and roll"? Well, another hit by Bill Haley and the band.

The deep influence of Bill Haley in rock and roll can only be seen with history's eyes since his massive hits created the perfect pathway for other artists to enter into the ears and hearts of a growing audience that needed more rock and roll songs to dance to and have fun.

Perhaps, Bill Haley & His Comets might be outdone by other acts that came after them, but they were very important in this first wave to open the path for other acts coming after them.

Fats Domino

Fats Domino's impact on the history of rock and roll is uncanny. Besides selling over 65 million records, he wrote some of the most iconic rock and roll songs of the first era. But it doesn't stop there, Elvis Presley talks about Domino as one of his biggest influences and so do the Beatles.

Hit songs like "The Fat Man" "Ain't That a Shame" and "Blueberry Hill", besides being inducted into the Grammy Hall of Fame set the foundations for what was coming. Moreover, it's hard to think of rock and roll without Fats Domino as part of the equation.

Funny enough, he never believed he was playing rock and roll; he stated publicly several times that he was playing rhythm and blues in the New Orleans style.

Elvis Presley

Ladies and gentlemen, get on your feet, please! It's time to introduce The King.

Yes, wherever he went, whatever he did, people referred to him as The King of Rock and Roll. This statement is true in many ways because there wasn't any other artist in the time of Elvis who propelled rock and roll into a more massive audience. Elvis broke all the rules on TV, dancing, singing, and taking the rock and roll culture, attitude, and music to a massive audience that was taken by surprise.

It was a scandal, it was brave, it was epic; it was rock and roll emerging from the king's voice.

Elvis Presley sold over 500 million records worldwide and helped spread the rock and roll revolution on both sides of the ocean. He was the king of rock and roll, a pioneer, and perhaps, its best-known singer to date.

Little Richard

Elvis was undoubtedly The King of Rock and Roll but Little Richard was known as The Architect of Rock and Roll. He helped shape everything that was to come starting with his 1955 megahit "Tutti Frutti", which we all heard and danced to more than once.

But beyond having his songs covered and recorded by all the greatest like Elvis, Buddy Holly, Bill Haley, and more, he was the crossover artist that brought together African-Americans and the white US population under the same beat. Indeed, he had 15 number-one hits between 1955 and 1962.

Furthermore, when touring Europe, his opening act was no other than The Beatles. Truth or myth, he's known for teaching Paul McCartney some of his wild vocalization techniques.

Little Richard was, perhaps, the most incendiary and charismatic rock and roll artist of all time and was named by Elvis Presley "the greatest".

Buddy Holly

Buddy Holly had a meteoric career with a sudden, too-early end in a plane crash in 1959.

Why is Buddy Holly on this list? Well, he was the first one to cement the two guitars, bass, and drums rock formation and toured the world (Australia and the UK at least) taking rock and roll beyond the boundaries of his nation.

Furthermore, artists the size of Bob Dylan, The Rolling Stones, The Beatles, Eric Clapton, Elvis Costello, and Elton John cite Buddy Holly as one of their strongest influences. Plus, if I can add, he was one of the few pioneers who rocked a sunburst Fender Stratocaster right after it was launched into the market.

Songs like "That'll be the day" and "Peggy Sue" will make his nerdy look, shy voice, and great guitar playing live forever.

What Instruments Propelled Rock N' Roll Forward?

Speaking about the Fender Stratocaster, let's get to know some of the most iconic guitars of this genre's evolution. Yes, it's time to get nerdy, technical, and into a topic we all love: musical instruments and gear.

We'll start with guitars and then move on to amplifiers. We'll leave drums out; it's just worth mentioning that the drum kit as we know it today was invented by the Ludwig Drum Company in 1918 under the name Jazz-Er-Up.

Also, an honorable mention to all the bass players out there, the foundational moment in musical history for rock bass players was 1951. That year, the Fender Company commercialized the first Fender Precision Bass, a version of the bass with frets that could be plugged in, and was easy to transport.

It started a revolution and made the dual-guitar, bass, and drums format possible for groups to travel and spread the rock and roll seed across the ocean and within every country in the world.

Let's Talk Styles And Sub-Genres

Meet My Personal Favorites!

Now that we've spoken about the place where rock and roll comes from and what guitars and amps helped in that trip, let me tell you who my all-time favorite bands and guitar players are.

My All-time Favorite Bands
» Red Hot Chili Peppers
» The White Stripes
» The Strokes
» Arctic Monkeys
» Black Sabbath
» The Ramones
» The Rolling Stones
» The Beatles
» Nirvana
» Pearl Jam

My All-time Favorite Guitar Players

» Jimi Hendrix

» Carlos Santana

» John Frusciante

» Jack White

» Dave Navarro

» Keith Richards

» John Mayer

» Kenny Wayne Shephard

» Stevie Ray Vaughan

» David Gilmour

Is Rock N' Roll Dead Or Is It Still A Thing In 2022?

I'm going to go with Alex Turner's initial words and say: Rock and Roll will never die.

Yes, it goes through popularity phases, just like everything else in our culture.

For example, have you ever realized that fashion is cyclic? The clothing that was hip at the beginning of the '90s is now trendy again.

Well, in my opinion, the same thing happens with music, especially, rock music. Rock music is constantly changing, morphing, mutating, associating, and moving forward. Yes, the number of rock and roll artists has grown after the pandemic with many new acts making exciting new music coming out every day.

Moreover, according to recent statistics, the number of guitars sold in 2020, when compared to 2019 raised 15%. This was mainly directed to the beginner section with brands like Fender and Gibson being among the best-sellers of the past decade.

But why is this important? Well, because there is no tighter bond in history than the one the guitar and rock and roll have. Of course, you can rock with a piano like Jerry Lee Lewis and Little Richard did, but the guitar is the perfect vessel for the genre's wild spirit and roaring sounds.

Perhaps, what we can say is that rock has mutated and given birth to a plethora of new generations of musicians that will play their hearts and souls to the instrument to bring their music forward.

This, in a world that is so overcrowded and flooded with information, makes it difficult to find the new great voices of this never-ending genre.

Nevertheless, it is we, rock players and fans that can keep it alive for time to come. We can do so by playing it, going to see new bands, investigating, buying records, and supporting the brand-new rockers of the next generations.

"Rock and roll will never die and there's nothing you can do about it." said rocking legend Alex Turner.

He is absolutely right, as long as there are players to push it forward, rock and roll will triumphantly sound forever.

What will it sound like in this decade? Well, we leave that to you because the best rock is always yet to come.

Are you ready to rock, rattle, and roll?

Welcome.

CHAPTER 1

Chords
Beyond Your Basic Open Chords

Chords are the unsung heroes of rock and roll. While all the eyes are on the lightning-speed fingers of the lead guitar player (we'll get there too, don't worry), the whole band is making it happen through a song structure made of chords.

In other words, without the proper chords, there is no rock and roll.

Let me tell you that, by writing this chapter, I'm having a flashback to my teenage years of Floyd Rose guitars and pink hair. Back then, I was trying to play the fastest that I could humanly play and learning all kinds of scales and licks to show off at the local pub.

It turned out that I was missing the point completely. I was feeding entirely on high hopes and thin air, overlooking the most important aspect of it: when and how to use these newly-acquired skills.

It was an older friend of mine who saved me. He sat down with me after a long jam in which I was soloing in the wrong key all night long. He said: "You're not listening; you need to pay attention to what's happening around you." Finally, he said to my weeping eyes: "You have to learn chords, first. Otherwise, it's all useless."

His words really got me and as soon as I could figure out what was all that chord mumbo jumbo I became a 300% better guitar player. So, I guess it's my turn now to pass it forward and teach you to lay the foundations to build your rocking sonic empire.

Go get your guitar, because here we go.

Chords Convey Emotions

Chords are the ones conveying the emotion in every song. Therefore, if you, for example, have a song with mostly minor chords, you'll be conveying sad feelings. On the other hand, if you are using major chords, you'll be communicating happiness and well-being.

Moreover, if you know where to use which, you'll create dynamics; one of the secrets to success.

So, let's take a look at how to use these emotions and colors to make people dance, shout, jump, scream, cry, or all of that together.

Most Used Chords In Rock Music

Rock music has historically been a simple, yet effective music style when compared to others like jazz. Hence, there are many, many songs written in only a handful of chords that have become stadium anthems.

The way we'll approach this topic is by tackling the most widely used ones first: major, minor, and power chords. After addressing those (which make for 90% of your needs), we'll get to the flavors and colors with other kinds of chords like 7th, dominants, diminished, and such.

Chord Construction

Chords are mostly triads. This means they are built utilizing three notes. For example, if we take the C major chord we can make it by combining C, G, and E. In the same vein, the G major chord is G, B, and D. So, as long as you know what the notes involved are, you know what chord is being played.

Speaking of which, let's dive right into the major chords.

Major Chords

Let's take a look at three different ways to construct major chords. These shapes can be found inside the CAGED system.

CAGED System

This system helps you to visualise how chords present themselves on the guitar. It's an excellent tool to navigate your fretboard by learning only 5 open chord shapes! C, A, G, E and D shapes hence the word CAGED.

And for you guys I have narrowed down even more. Just learn only 3 shapes and you can play any song with them. Well rock and pop songs.

C Major Chord

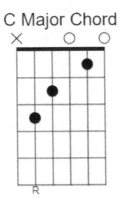

B Major Chord

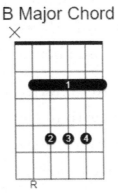

F Major Chord

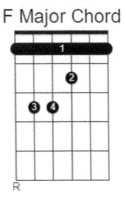

Let's dissect the shapes we've formed so you can use them to make any chord you want anywhere on the fretboard.

F Major Chord (CAGED System Position 4)

This shape is one of the first bar chords we learn on guitar. The root note of the chord is on the 6th string, hence, knowing what that note is, you can move the same shape and make that major chord anywhere on the fretboard. For example, if we moved the F Major Chord to the 5th fret, we can make an A major chord. Likewise, moving it to the 10th fret will transform it into a D Major.

B Major Chord (CAGED System Position 2)

The shape of this major chord finds its root note on the 5th string. Thus, moving the shape around the fretboard creates the major chord the root note dictates. So, for example, moving it to the 5th fret creates a D Major. Likewise, moving it one semitone up to the 3rd fret will give you a C major.

C Major Chord (CAGED System Position 1)

Finally, the C major chord is the first position of the CAGED system. Thus, maintaining the same shape and moving it down the fretboard (fretting the open strings with your index finger) can help you find a major chord wherever you want on the fretboard. Always remember that the note on the 5th string will give you the root, and hence, the name of the chord.

This was the secret for Oasis to break through, for example. This is an inside tip, no chord sounds bigger than the first-position open chords with those roaring open strings. Therefore, learning the open positions for every chord can be the key to unlocking amazing choruses.

This is an example of it:

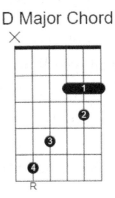

Minor Chords

While major chords can help you bring crowds to sing along on a massive chorus, minor chords will help you build the tension and create the space for the big major chords to drop. In other words, if you can't create dynamics and contrast, you'll never be able to generate momentum for big choruses to explode.

Moreover, minor chords can make tears, cell phone screens, and emotion flood the venue.

So, learning how to create minor chords is a must if you want to learn how to convey emotions in a song. But before you get the crowds singing and going bananas on your latest hit, you need to learn the shapes.

Let's take a look at three minor shapes just like we did with major shapes.

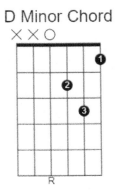
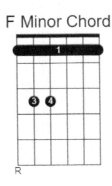
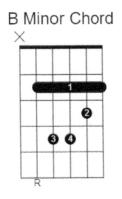

F Minor Chord (Minor CAGED System Position 4)

Just like we've seen for the F major chord, as long as you move the entire shape up and down the fretboard, you'll always get a minor chord with the root on the 6th string. If you move it to fret 2 (back a semitone), for example, you'll be constructing an open E minor.

B Minor Chord (Minor CAGED System Position 2)

The same example as above but on the 5th string. So, as long as you move the same chord shape up and down the fretboard, you can name the chord with the note you're fretting on the 5th string (the root). For example, if you move it one tone down, you'll get the open A minor chord.

D Minor Chord (Minor CAGED System Position 5)

As the last position of the Minor CAGED System, if you move this shape down the fretboard and fret the root note (open D in this case), you can construct any minor chord you like anywhere on the fretboard. Remember that the fretted root note will give you the name of the chord.

For example, moving the shape one tone up will give us an E minor (Em). It looks something like this:

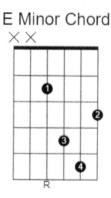

E Minor Chord

Power Chords

Power chords are the backbone of many musical styles related to rock and roll. Furthermore, they are the only chord shape used by many headlining bands in popular songs.

For example, if you happen to like any Punk Rock bands like the Ramones, you can play most of their records utilizing only power chords.

Another name for power chords can be 5ths because they are made of the root note and its 5th. Yes, just like it sounds, it is that simple. And yes, Johnny Ramone and his friends created an entire sonic revolution utilizing those simple notes.

Let's take the F power chord as an example. We're going to use the root note, F, and add the 5th note, which is C.

This is what the F power chord looks like:

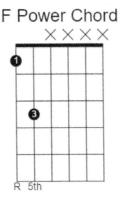

F Power Chord

Very easy, right? Well, it gets even better, because as long as you move the same shape, your index finger will always dictate the root note. So, for example, if you move your index to the third fret and your ring finger to your fourth fret, you'll have a G power chord.

G Power Chord

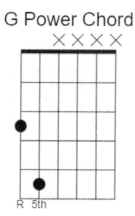

Although that is the quintessential shape, it can be modified to make it sound fuller or add colors to the shape. For example, we can add the 8ve or 9th note to it.

8ve is short form of octave. For example:

F Power Chord

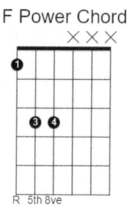

By adding the 8ve, your chord will sound fuller, and, since you're repeating the root note, the chord will not change its color or power, it will just sound bigger.

Another common change to this shape is adding the 9th to your power chord which makes it perfect for arpeggios, fattening the sound, and making anything sound heavier when you add distortion.

This is what a power chord with the added 9th looks like:

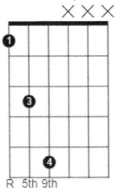

F Power Chord (added 9th)

Octaves

What happens if we remove the 5th note from the above chord? You get octaves that sound great in melodic lines, especially when distorted. Octaves made this simple way look something like this:

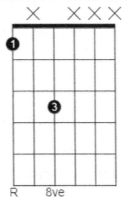

F Octave Power Chord

Some song examples where this technique is used for you to hear are:

- » "The Immigrant Song" (Led Zeppelin)
- » "The Wanton Song" (Led Zeppelin)
- » "My Sharona" (The Knack)
- » "Bulls on Parade"(Rage Against The Machine)
- » "Purple Haze / Easy Rider" (Jimi Hendrix)

The one caveat about this shape is that it changes to accommodate the 2nd string's note. So, octaves on the 5th and 4th string look something like this:

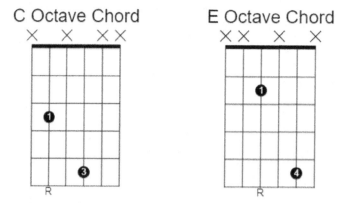

Here Come The Flavors (Other Chord Shapes)

While it is true that most of rock n roll is done around the major, minor, and power chords, many other shapes can be ear-catching flavors to keep your listeners engaged. Furthermore, there are a plethora of examples of how introducing an element from another genre can change a song completely making it more appealing.

For example, take "Kashmir" by Led Zeppelin with that ethnic feeling, or "Sympathy for the Devil" by The Rolling Stones. Still, this resource can be a much softer touch like in "(Can't get no) Satisfaction" by The Rolling Stones with an iconic B7 in the intro that generates tension.

These chords work great for creating tension and building momentum making the listener wait for the resolving phrases. Although we're going to go deeper into them in our next chapter when we talk about chord progressions, here are some of the most useful ones you need to learn to take your rock n roll compositions to stardom level.

As I write these lines I can still hear my friend's voice saying: "All the info you need is in the chords.". He was right; once I learned how to use that info, I became a much better guitar player and musician.

That will happen to you too; take my word for it.

Dominant 7th Chords (V7)

To form a dominant chord you need to add a note to the triad. Remember that we built our major chords utilizing a triad that was a root note, the 3rd, and the 5th? Well, to build a dominant 7th chord, we're going to add another note: a flat 7th (also called "dominant 7th").

Let's pour this into an example to make it easier. Let's say we have a C major chord, (C + E + G). We want to make that a dominant 7th so we add a flat 7th to it (Bb).

Our dominant 7th will look something like this:

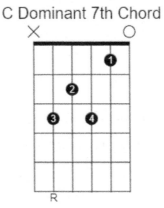

C Dominant 7th Chord

We'll see more of its use in detail in the following chapter, but it's useful to say no other chord (in this list at least) generates as much tension screaming for a release as this chord does.

Major 7th Chords

Major 7th chords fulfill a similar duty as dominant 7th chords but aren't so drastic; they feel a tad softer to the ear. Therefore, we can use them to create an atmosphere without feeling claustrophobic.

The way we form a major 7th chord is very similar to the way we form a dominant 7th chord. This time, instead of using a flat 7th, we shall use a 7th. So, if we go back to our example using the C major chord (C, G, E) and we add the 7th (B) we get a chord formed like this: C, G, E, B.

Let's see what that looks like:

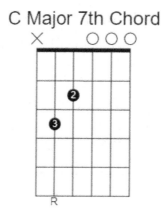

Also, if you want to move it around and form other chords, as long as you remember the tonic, you can move it using your index finger to make for the open strings.

For example, a D Major 7th chord can look something like this:

D Major 7th Chord

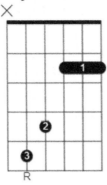

Minor 7th Chords

Minor 7th chords are super special because they can captivate the audience by mixing two ingredients we had already used before: minor and 7th. Therefore, utilizing a chord like this can instantly turn any song into a powerful ballad, Moreover it's a great twist to any chord progression to keep everyone expecting what will happen next.

How do we construct such a chord? Well, let's take our C major chord again (C, E, G). Now, let's turn it into a minor chord by flattening the third: E turns into Eb. Now, let's add the fourth note to make it a 7th. In this case, we need to add a flattened 7th (Bb).

The result is C, Eb, G, Bb. Let's see what that looks like:

C Minor 7th Chord

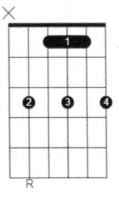

Moving these chords around the fretboard, keeping their shape, and minding the root note will give you the same minor 7th chord everywhere on the fretboard.

For example, the D minor 7th chord looks something like this:

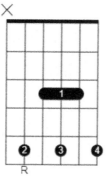

Diminished Chords

Diminished chords have a very particular, sad, melancholic, "sweet & sour" tone that makes them very unique. So unique that they can spice up any meal; they are the ingredient that shows you're a chef and not just a cook. Let's see how they can add flavor to your rocking compositions.

Some examples of songs with diminished chords are:

> » "Purple Rain" (Prince)
> » "I Want You (She's so Heavy)" (The Beatles)
> » "Rock this Town" (The Stray Cats)
> » "Now You Can Tell" (Chuck Berry)

But how do I play a diminished chord?

Well, to create a diminished chord we need to stick to the following formula:

Root note - Minor 3rd - Diminished 5th.

Let's translate that into an example taking our beloved C chord again. The root note is C, the minor 3rd is D#, and the diminished 5th is F#.

It looks something like this:

C - D# - F#

Here are three different versions of how this chord should look like on your guitar:

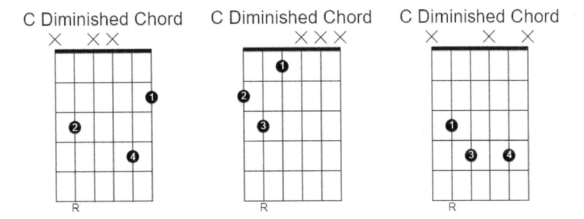

Just like in the previous examples, since these shapes don't have any open strings ringing, you can move them around and form other diminished chords minding the root note you're fretting on the 5th string.

Minor 7th b5th chords

The last chord we'll be looking at for this chapter is the minor 7th flat 5th or half-diminished chord. But beware, because this is not just another chord (insert macabre laughing). Jokes aside, it is a great flavor to add to any progression that has a minor 7h chord in it. How so? Well, you can just flatten the 5th and give the progression a new flavor with a single changed note.

Yes, it is that simple; its name implies everything.

Let's take a look at the formula to create a minor 7th chord with the addition of a flat 5th:

Root note - flat 3rd - flat 5th - flat 7th

If we pour this inside a chord structure, for example, C, we'll get:

C - Eb - Gb - Bb

Let's see what that shape looks like on a guitar neck:

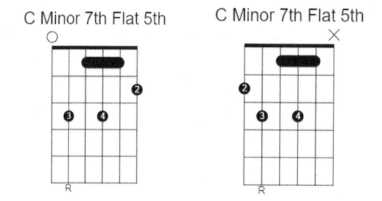

Finally, you can move the shape throughout the neck as long as you keep in mind where the root note is. Here's what a D min7th flat 5th (or half-diminished) looks like:

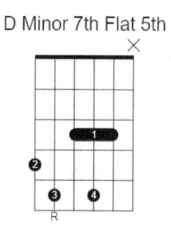

In the words of a Jedi Master: "Master the chords you will, and the rocking universe yours will be."

So, go practice, master the chords, and we'll see each other in the next chapter to turn them into songs by organizing them into famous progressions.

> I realized by using the high notes of the chords as a melodic line, and by the right harmonic progression, I could play what I heard inside me. That's when I was born.
>
> **- Charlie Parker**

CHAPTER 2

Most Used Chord Progressions
Use Them To Write Your Song

Now that you know chords, it is time to make them do their magic. Hence, we're going to take this explanation one step further and talk about intervals and chord progressions.

Intervals are the spaces between the notes and these intervals generate what we know as music. For example, if you are a singer or have friends who sing, you'll often hear them singing songs in "a comfortable key". This means you can change a song's key as long as you maintain its intervals and listeners will recognize it anyways.

Moreover, each interval or chord progression will make the listener feel a certain way. Thus, once you know the most famous chord progressions, where they come from, and what they generate in the audience, you'll be able to make your own and touch more people with your music.

Therefore, in this chapter, we'll go over rock's most used chord progressions and dissect them to understand why they work the way they work. After turning known songs into tools, we'll leave a space so you can come up with your own chord progression and/or first rock and roll song.

Go get that guitar of yours because here we go!

Famous Rock N Roll Chord Progressions With Examples

Beginning Of The Rock And Roll Revolution: I-IV-V-I Chord Progression

Let's begin by taking a look at one of the most famous chord progressions of all time: I-IV-V-I. This chord progression was widely used by pioneers in the 50s and 60s.

Some song examples for this chord progression could be:

» "Like a Rolling Stone" (Bob Dylan)
» "Born to Run" (Bruce Springsteen)
» "Rock and Roll All Nite" (Kiss)
» "Mr. Jones" (Simon and Garfunkel)

It's a great chord progression by itself, but we can make it work even better. Indeed, if we turn the V chord into a 7th, the progression urges us to go back to the I.

$$I - IV - V - I = E - A - B7 - E$$

This chord progression was The Beatles' secret for songs such as "Twist and Shout" and "Lucy in the Sky with Diamonds".

First, we'll see the chords we'll use, and then we'll put together the progression.

Chords are:

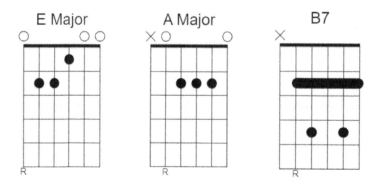

Now the progression looks something like this:

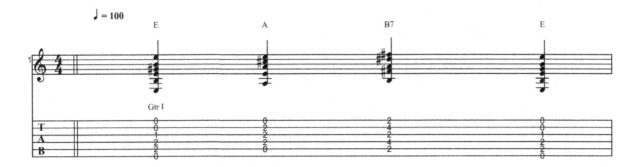

> You'll find the track to hear what it sounds like in our bonus material.

The Emotional Side Of Rock And Roll: I-V-VI-IV Chord Progression

The intervals between chords generate a particular atmosphere or emotional state. In that regard, no other chord progression goes so far into sentimental territory as this one does. Yes, this chord progression unveils the emotional side of rock and roll and is a highway straight to your listeners' hearts.

ROMAN NUMERALS

Roman Numerals identify the scale degree of the chord's root, the chord's quality, and any extensions or inversions the chord may include. For example,

- » In the key of C, V chord means G chord. G is the 5th degree of the scale hence V.
- » Uppercase Roman numerals represent major chords, while lowercase numerals represent minor chords.
- » Extremely useful system to memorize chord progression, and especially when are transposing it different keys.

Some song examples could be:

» "With or without you" (U2)
» "When I come around" (Green Day)
» "Bullet with butterfly wings" (Smashing Pumpkins)
» "It's my life" (Bon Jovi)
» "Otherside" (Red Hot Chili Peppers)

Let's see it in an example so we can clarify how it works. We'll use the key of C to make it simpler:

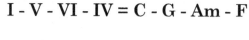

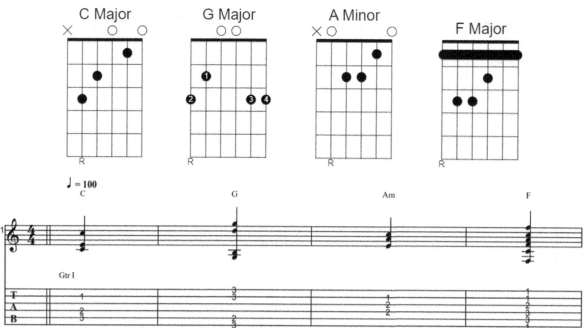

The Stadium Sing-along: VI-I-V-II Chord Progression

Stadium sing-alongs aren't just luck; there is a formula behind the magic that makes thousands of people want to jump, shout, scream, wave t-shirts, and pay for overpriced tickets. That formula is the one we are about to see and has been used to create some of the biggest anthems in modern music.

Some songs with this chord progression are:

- » "Radioactive" (Imagine Dragons)
- » "Detroit Rock" City (Kiss)
- » "Wonderwall" (Oasis)
- » "Boulevard of Broken Dreams" (Green Day)
- » "Pumped Up Kicks" (Foster the People)

Perhaps, the most recognizable of them all is that modern version of "Let it Be" that all of us who were born post-Beatles think "Wonderwall" by Oasis is.

But how do we put together this powerful combination of sounds and emotions? Well, let's take a look at the formula poured into our beloved key of C:

VI - I - V - II = Am - C - G - Dm

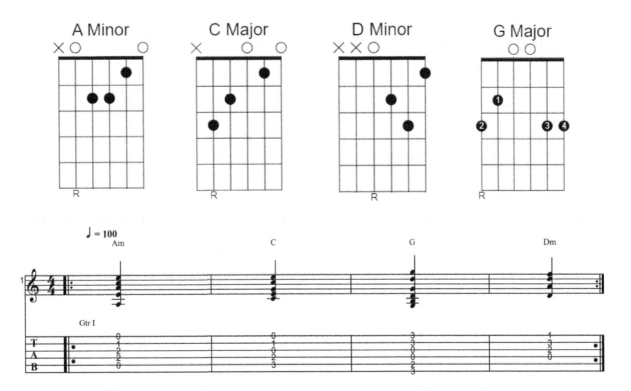

The Golden Secret To Mainstream Hits: VI- IV- I- V Chord Progression

Doesn't it happen to you when you spend time listening to casual music passively, like in a cafe, or a bar, that most hit songs sound alike? I mean despite production techniques, different flavors, instrumentation, lyrics, and key selection, they all sound somewhat familiar, don't they?

Well, you're not a nut case going to the cuckoo's nest; on the contrary, you've discovered the golden secret: this chord progression has fueled many hit songs taking them straight to the top of the charts.

But why is this chord progression so catchy? Well, the reason why these intervals work together so perfectly is that when you strike the first minor VI chord you set the mood for a deep, heartfelt melody but by the time you've reached the root note, the I chord, you're in upbeat heaven. Finally, you can add a 7th note to the V chord and resolve to the VI easily.

Some sample songs with this chord progression are:

- » "Electrical Storm" (U2)
- » "Little Talks" (Of Monsters and Men)
- » "Numb" (Linkin Park)
- » "Snow (Hey Oh)" (Red Hot Chili Peppers)
- » "The Kids Aren't Alright" (The Offspring)

There is a strong emotional, touchy side to this chord progression that matches perfectly with a "stadium anthem" quality.

Let's make an example of the best-kept secret among best-selling musicians in the world using the Key of C to make it easier.

$$VI - IV - I - V = Am - F - C - G$$

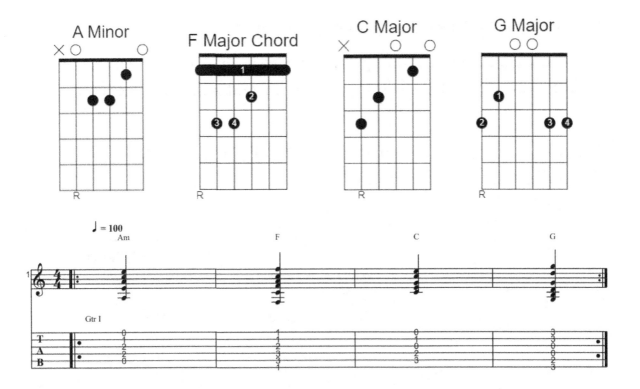

The All-Time Standard: The 12-Bar Blues Progression

If you are out, jamming with a bunch of musicians you'll very likely come across this chord progression. Moreover, the perfect way to get the chemistry started when you're playing with fellow musicians for the first time is to play a 12-bar blues in the singer's most comfortable key.

The version we are going to review in this book is the standard, basic, quintessential progression that will get you through most jam sessions.

But jam sessions aren't the only environment where this progression is paramount, it has fueled countless hits throughout the years. Let's see some song examples utilizing this chord progression:

» "Born under a bad sign" (Albert King)
» "Something like Olivia" (John Mayer)
» "Mustang Sally" (Wilson Picket)
» "Johnny B Goode" (Chuck Berry)
» "Hound Dog" (Elvis Presley)

But how does the 12-bar blues progression work?

Well, for starters, it is a 12-bar progression so it's a structure that's repeated every 12 bars. Therefore, you need to count and start back again when it ends.

The progression involves 3 degrees: I - IV - V. Let's see what it looks like with the Key of C to make it simpler:

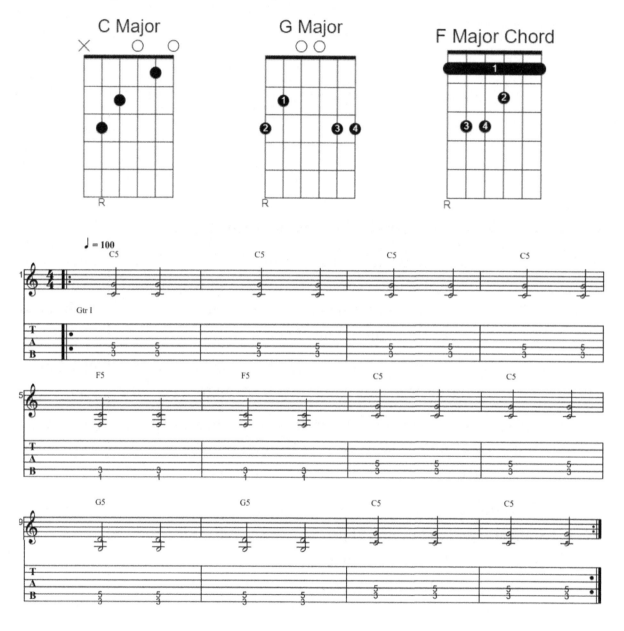

Let's spice up the chord shapes by adding a note. That little detail makes it impossible not to think of rock n roll when you play it.

C Power Chord Variation

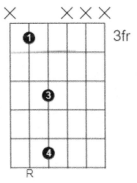

The idea here is to use the 3rd and 4th fingers interchangeably during your playing. We're going to go for a particular picking pattern that involves only downstrokes in the following shape, let's take a look:

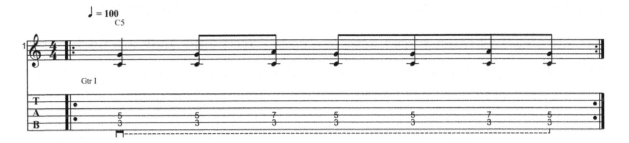

As the chord above works the same way as every power chord (you do remember from chapter 1, right?) you can move it around and use the same pattern to achieve a similar effect in every chord.

Blues on, Garth!

The Odd Flavor of Rock Going Massive: The I-bVII-IV Chord Progression

When Rock finally made it out of its initial phase of being Blues' little (and kind of dumb) brother, new flavors appeared on the radio. This was a phenomenon, especially during the '60s and '70s in which massive rock acts like The Who, The Rolling Stones, Queen, Aerosmith, and many others started playing.

During this time, musicians went after borrowed chords that could give their compositions something else, different, like the I - bVII - IV chord progression we're about to see.

Let's take a look at some examples:

> "Sweet Home Alabama" (Lynyrd Skynyrd)
> "Sweet child o' mine" (Guns n' Roses)
> "Won't get fooled again" (The Who)
> "Hush" (Deep Purple)
> "Magic Bus" (The Who)

Most of these songs have become part of the sonic DNA of many of us because they had this trick hidden inside: a borrowed chord. Indeed, it is this slight difference that makes them as unique as they are appealing to the masses.

Writing this and seeing "Sweet child o' mine" in the list took me back to my music store days. Whenever anyone, of any age, asked for a Les Paul guitar, we all knew what was going to happen. Yes, I've heard that song more than any other in my life. Furthermore, I heard it being played amazingly well, amazingly bad, with a solo, sung, instrumental, without the solo, and in any other combination, you might think of; I even heard it on a ukulele once!

But enough with memories and theory, let's have some fun. Let's pour the C key inside this empty structure and see what we can come up with.

I - bVII - IV = C - Bb - F

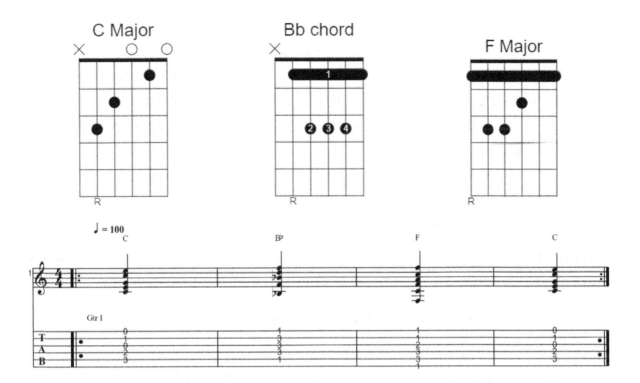

The Guitar Hero Anthem: The II - V - I - IV Chord Progression

In February 2011, the world lost a guitar hero, a man who inspired generations of musicians to go back into the blues and transform it once again. Indeed, if you've ever seen or heard Mr. Gary Moore play, you probably know that few other guitar players on this planet can sound so huge, accurate, melodic, and heavy at the same time.

What we are about to see is a chord progression that can be found in many of his songs. This chord progression borrows from two neighboring styles: blues and pop. So, it sounds rocking and powerful but also emotional, dark, and catchy.

These songs feature this chord progression:

- » "Still got the Blues" (Gary Moore)
- » "Europa" (Santana)
- » "I Will Survive" (Gloria Gaynor)

In "Still got the blues", Gary Moore utilizes mostly 7th and minor chords for the progression to give it a crying/bluesy feel. Remember from chapter 1 that chords convey emotions and add colors to music? Well, this is a great example of that. This song is a bleeding blues anthem that gets to your heart in the first note and won't let you go until the massive 80s echo of the snare is done ringing.

Let's try and pour it over our trusty C major key to see what happens.

$$II - V - I - IV = Dm - G - C - F$$

This is one of the possible variations that can sound pop and of joy. What Gary plays in "Still got the blues" is this:

$$II - V - I - IV = Dm7 - G11 - Cmaj7 - Fmaj7$$

These added colors with bluesy chords make the song more epic, sad, and desperate. The entire chord progression in Gary's song is:

$$II - V - I - IV - VII - III - VI = Dm7 - G11 - Cmaj7 - Fmaj7 - Bm7b5 - E7 - Am7$$

As you can see from the song structure you can't find any major chords meaning the tension never resolves.

These are the chords of the simple progression:

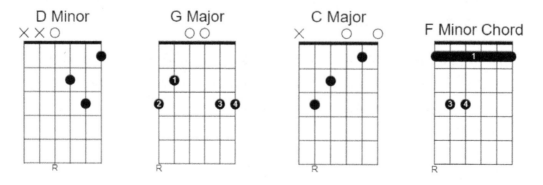

These are the chords if you want to play it as Gary plays it:

Bm7b5   **Dm7 Chord**   **G11 Chord**

C Maj 7   **F Maj 7**   **E7 Chord**

Half Cadence Or Incomplete Cadence: The I - V - Ii - V Chord Progression

There is something about a half cadence that is perfect to use as a hook and keep people into the music with a happy, relaxed feeling. This happens because this progression resolves to the V, hence, it keeps the tension accumulating instead of resolving to the I which releases it. Furthermore, you can exchange the II for an IV and get a different flavor in a similar cadence.

Perhaps, the best way to explain this effect is with Scorpions' "Wind of change". We all agree it is an '80s anthem that we've been singing forever that could have 20 choruses one next to the other and we would sing them all. This is because of this progression's hypnotic loop of "never resolving".

Let's take a look at what it looks like with our beloved key of C:

$$\text{I - V - II - V = C - G - Dm - G}$$

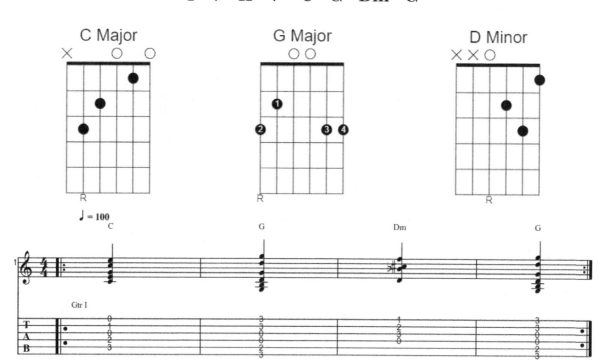

The Effortless Descend On A Sad Note: The VI - V - IV Chord Progression

We've just seen the benefits of the beautiful I - V half-cadence progression leaving the open space for endless repetition. But what would happen if we replaced that almighty I or root note with its relative minor or VI? Well, starting the progression with a minor chord adds a gloomy atmosphere to whatever we're playing.

But from that sad VI, we go to the V and then keep on descending to the IV which allows for cool descending bass lines and gives the listener a sense of being "trapped" in the melody.

These are some songs that benefit from this chord progression:

- » "Under My Thumb" (The Rolling Stones)
- » "All Along the Watchtower" (Bob Dylan)
- » "Dream On" (Aerosmith)
- » "Stop In The Name of Love" (The Supremes)

Let's take a look at what it looks like if we use our beloved key of C for it. We'll add the resolution Aerosmith uses in "Dream On" which is going back to the V.

<h3 style="text-align:center">VI - V - IV - V = Am - G - F - G</h3>

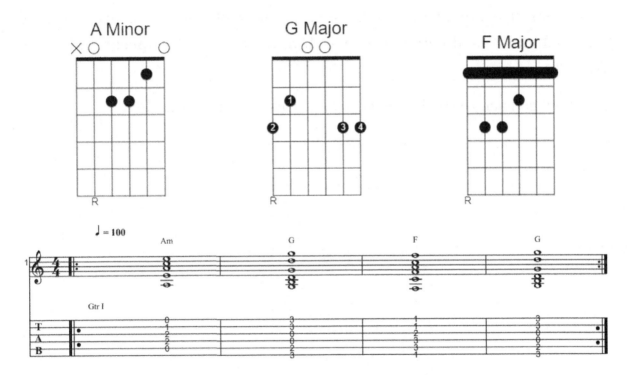

There is a very famous variation to this chord progression that is called by music connoisseurs the "Andalusian cadence". This cadence retains that sweet and sour feeling but adds a III to finish it making it more uplifting and hit-friendly.

Here are some examples of historical hit songs that benefit from the Andalusian cadence:

- » "Hit the Road, Jack" (Ray Charles)
- » "Babe, I'm Gonna Leave You" (Led Zeppelin)
- » "China Girl" (David Bowie)
- » "Like a Hurricane" (Neil Young)
- » "Sultans of Swing" (Dire Straits)

Perhaps, the best-known of them is "Sultans of Swing" by Dire Straits, a band commanded by one of the most resourceful guitar players of all time and a master finger picker, Mark Knopfler.

You can easily recognize how the descending guitar and bass line establish a conversation giving the whole song a sense of being weightless while also including a sad note to the overall flavor that's kept upbeat and radio friendly.

So, if we go back to the key of C to pour this into an example:

VI - V - IV - III = Am - G - F - Em

E Minor Chord

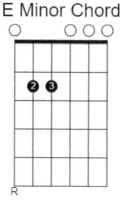

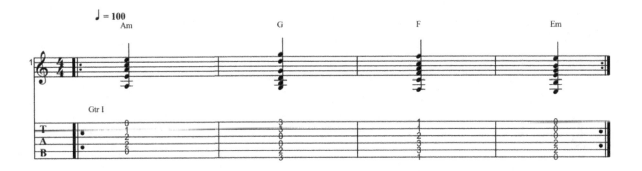

It's Your Turn To Write A Chord Progression

This is your space in the book to write down your first chord progression. Moreover, we're going to do this formally, with space for chords and notation.

This is the simple set of steps to follow:

1. Pick a chord progression we've covered in this chapter.
2. Choose a key that's suitable for you.
3. Transform the structure into chords.
4. Write down the progression.
5. Write down the chords you'll use
6. Use the pentagram and TAB for your new creation

Your Chord progression:

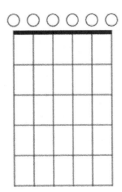 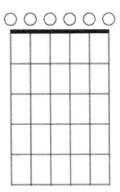 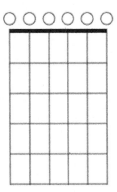

I thrive on change. That's probably why my chord changes are weird, because chords depict emotions. They'll be going along on one key and I'll drop off a cliff, and suddenly they will go into a whole other key signature. That will drive some people crazy, but that's how my life is..

- Joni Mitchell

CHAPTER 3

Rhythm Guitar
That's How A Pro Comps

Guitar players need to divide their brains into two sides: the left hand and the right hand.

I remember very clearly how I learned why my picking hand was just as important as my fretting hand. I was playing guitar over all the records I could find, picking out solos by ear. Suddenly, one of the speakers blew up and started making only rattle sounds. So, I used the "balance" knob to hear the music on the working side.

To my disappointment, the mix only had the bass, drums, and rhythm guitar on that channel. The lead guitar was gone. After recovering from the bummer, I started hearing what bass, rhythm guitar, and drums mean for a song, and playing to that made me a much better guitar player.

That is exactly what you'll get from this chapter, enough information and exercises to master that picking hand of yours.

Ready to get started? Go get your guitar because

Here We Go!

The Overdriven Open Chords - Rock N Roll In Its Pure Form

Perhaps you're an AC-DC fan too. I know I've been following the Young brothers ever since the first time I heard "TNT" on the radio. I remain a hardcore fan to this day; they kept me hooked from day one.

But what is the trick? How do we do what AC-DC does with our instruments and hands to build a legion of hardcore fans? Well, the name of the game is "Syncopation". This is not a guitar technique, it is borrowed from the drumming universe.

What syncopation means, is to accentuate riffs and chords in offbeat positions. This way, the rhythm over which the melody, lead work, and solos sit is dynamic, interesting, and keeps the band in a constant "rolling forward" feeling for the listener.

This syncopation is achieved by utilizing the offbeat accents, and staccato beats mixed with pauses, gaps, and full stops.

To begin with, let's make a chord progression so we can fit it into our rhythm pattern. You know how this is done, so we won't go over the mechanism again.

Our first chord progression is a very simple one:

$$E - A - G - D = II - V - IV - I$$

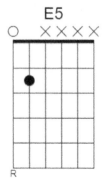
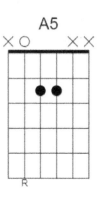

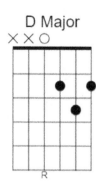

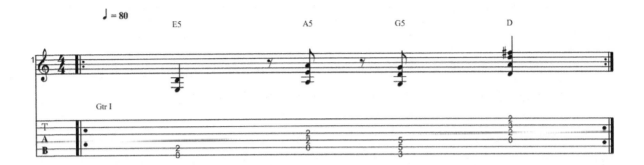

Notice how the 8th rests work to create syncopation and the stress is not in the first beat but in the second. This is not random or casual, it's the band's signature sound.

Let's try and expand this concept by utilizing something that's another trademark by AC-DC which is to add notes between the chords. We're going to add another chord we're borrowing from the key of Ab; C5.

The pro tip I can give you is to pay attention to the figures and the notes; in that order. Remember, it is a rhythmic exercise.

You'll find the track to hear what it sounds like in our bonus material.

Power Chords! Louder, POWER CHORDS!

If a rocker was to go to a desert island and could only take one type of chord in his or her suitcase, 100% will agree to take power chords.

Yes, power chords are the beef, the potatoes, and also the gravy for rock n rollers.

We already saw them in chapter one. If you don't remember them, this is the perfect moment to go back and refresh that knowledge.

In this section, we'll cover three techniques you can use with your right hand and keep power chords varied, dynamic, and always interesting. So, this is not just a lesson, it is a thunderous new power you're about to unlock.

Plus, you'll probably play power chords for your entire musical life. So, ready or not, just like Punk Rock, here we go.

Exercise 1

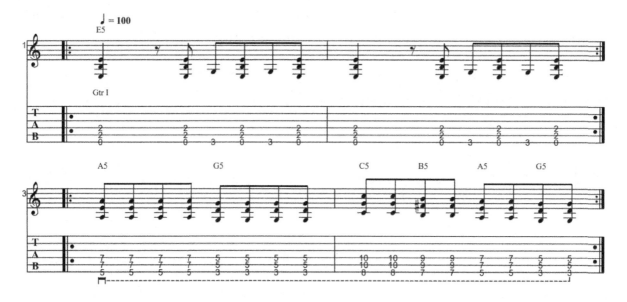

The first bar involves the E5 chord or E power chord with a slight variation: we add a low G to the mix. This note added to the chord will create a heavy sound. For the second section of the exercise, we'll practice down-picking over power chords.

Note that all of these chords in the exercise are played using downstrokes only and in 8th notes. We'll call this "the Johnny Ramone pattern" because it was one of the secrets to his uncanny sound.

Exercise 2

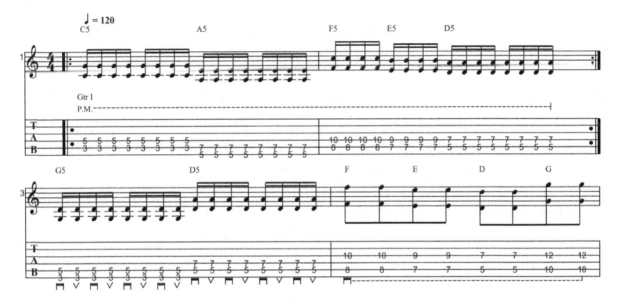

This exercise is great for learning two different skills: one is palm muting and the other one is playing 8ves in a power chord riff. Octaves, (when you remove the 5th note) can create a sudden melody that takes any riff to another level.

But first things first; let's talk about palm muting.

To achieve this effect, you need to place the palm of your hand on the strings you want to mute. While holding the palm down on them, you have to use the pick to pluck them. The sound should be a low-frequency "chug".

Once you've mastered the first part of the exercise with the downstroke palm muting, it is time to turn the verse into a chorus. So, use up-and-down strokes for the chorus letting strings ring freely.

Finally, we have added octaves to the mix just to make it more interesting. They make a small melody that could be the perfect canvas for killer lyrics.

All the shapes and theories for power chords are in the 1st chapter.

Your Fingers Are The Answer - Fingerpicking Rocking Arpeggios

The name of the game in this part of the chapter is going to be *fingerpicking*. That is because we'll break away from the pick for a while and try to figure out how to create a continuous loop by playing with our fingers.

The best part of learning fingerpicking techniques is that you can create 2 or 3-note combinations by pulling more than one string at a time. Two examples of fingerpicking arpeggios could be Leonard Cohen's "Suzanne" and the utterly known "Hotel California" by The Eagles.

But beyond examples, learning how to master pick and fingers is like unlocking a new skill in a video game. All of the sudden, you can get more sounds from the guitar than ever before.

These are some players who play exclusively with their fingers:

- » Mark Knopfler
- » Robbie Krieger (The Doors)
- » Chet Atkins
- » Jeff Beck
- » Derek Trucks
- » Richie Kotzen

Also, some players employ a mixed approach and alternate between fingers and pick. This gives their playing enhanced dynamics. Some examples are:

- » John Mayer
- » Jimi Hendrix (do teeth add as a non-conventional playing approach?)
- » Eric Clapton
- » Guthrie Govan
- » Eric Johnson
- » Rory Gallagher

But first things first, let's learn how to arpeggiate with the fingers.

So, let's think of our right hand as a picking instrument and name our fingers with numbers.

» Thumb = 0
» Index finger = 1
» Middle finger = 2
» Ring finger = 3
» Small finger = 4

As a rule of thumb, your thumb will be the one playing the low 3 strings (D, A, and E in regular tuning) while the rest of the fingers will play the first three (G, B, and E).

Exercise 1

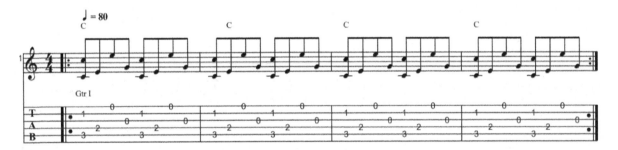

In this exercise, the 0 finger is for the 5th string, your 1 finger should play the E on the 4th string, the 3 finger should play the open E on the 1st string, and the 2 finger should play the open G.

Exercise 2

Now that we've got the basics down, it is time to introduce a chord progression and spice your fingerpicking up.

I - VI - II - V = C - Am - Dm - G

For the last chord of the exercise, you'll find a different shape, a new way of playing the G major that is more friendly with the strings we've been playing.

This new chord shape is played like this:

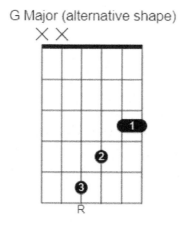

This is exercise number 2:

This is exercise number 3:

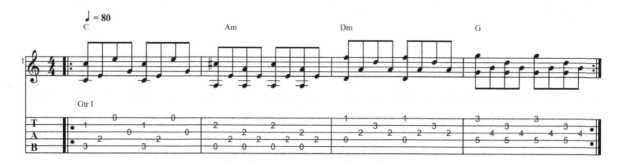

At first, your brain makes it difficult to identify and make each finger move independently. Don't get frustrated; making that connection is exactly the aim of the exercise.

So, for example, when you are playing the Dm you should use 0 and 1 fingers for the first notes, then fingers 2 and 3, and then 0 and 1 again.

> **PRO TIP:** Playing in a rock band does not mean you get to play solo every time and do your own thing. You are required to comp the singer or contribute to the song. Fail to do so and you'll risk getting fired from the band.

This is a lesson that will sound great played on an archtop guitar such as a Gibson ES-335. That will give it the body and low-end needed to make it stand on its own.

In The Name Of The Rock N Roll Pioneer - This Is How Chuck Berry Started It All

Arguably, without the presence of a guitar player of the caliber of Chuck Berry in the history of modern music, there wouldn't have been the Rolling Stones, Beatles, or many other rock n roll acts.

Indeed, Chuck Berry inaugurated not only a playing style but also a way to present music on stage. If you've ever watched Back to the Future, you surely remember Marty McFly's line: "Guess you guys aren't ready for this, but your kids are gonna love it".

That is how Chuck Berry's style felt for the people at the time: futuristic, one-of-a-kind playing.

This effect was achieved by Chuck Berry with his right hand, syncopating with the rest of the instruments of the band. That syncopation created a dancing mood among the audience.

To exercise this kind of playing, we'll use two new chord shapes that use the ring finger to play the added note. They are variations of A5 and E5, chords we have already seen.

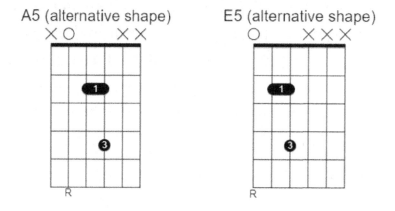

Exercise 1

This exercise is all about Chuck Berry's playing style: mixing small, two-note riffs, with a very simple chord progression with the right rhythm pattern.

Finally, the guitar Chuck used to show the world a new music style was a Gibson ES-345. That being said, this is a riff that can be played on any guitar as long as you add a little overdrive to it.

Keep it interesting! Introducing Slash Chords

Slash chords are, in simple words, chords in which the bass note (the lowest sound heard in the chord) is different from the root note.

For example, the C chord is C, E, and G. The lowest note in the chord is the root note: C.

But what if we changed that low note for another in the chord, like, for example, G. That chord would be called C/G. This formula works like this:

Chord name/Bass note

But, at this moment you might be scratching the top of your head with a pick, holding the guitar, and thinking: "Why is this important to become a Rhythm Master?". Well, the answer is very simple, you can hear examples of slash notes making chord progressions smoother in most songs within the top 10 charts in any style, but particularly rock and pop.

For example, the chord progression I - VI - II - V chord progression requires big jumps among the low notes of the chords. If we were to pour our beloved C major key into this structure, we would get:

I - VI - II - V = C - Am - Dm - G

So, from C to Am, the bass has to move 9 semitones. What if we could add a note in the middle to make the transition smoother? It doesn't have to be a note from the chord but any note that matches our needs. For example, we could play a G before the A and F# before G.

In our chord progression, it might look something like this:

C - C/G - Am - Dm - Dm/F# - G

This subtle but meaningful trick will help you add dynamics to your playing.

Let's see the chord shapes and then turn our chord progression into an exercise:

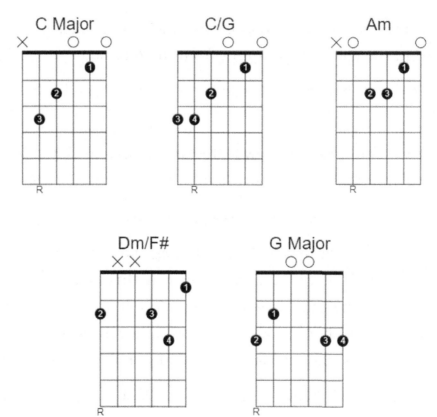

Exercise 1

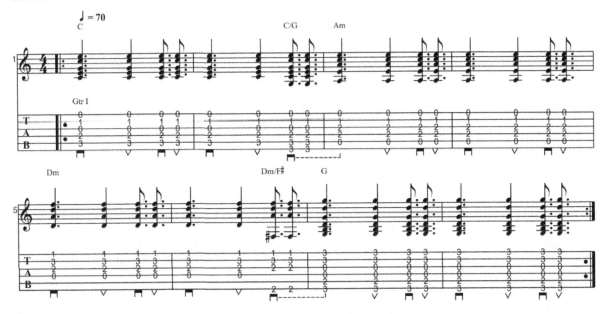

Rhythm-wise there are two main aspects to this exercise:

> » The use of dots for the figures
> » The particular up and down stroke patterns

The dots in the figures change the landing time for some of the chords that need to start with an upward movement of the pick. That will loosen up your right hand and make you a more interesting rhythm partner for any player.

Rock Goes Acoustic, Revising The Acoustic Style Of Pete Townshend

In my opinion, Pete Townshend is one of the most underrated rhythmic guitar players on Earth. Although his playing was a premonition to much of what came after, not many people in the guitar world seem to pay attention to his savage guitar playing style.

Well, we are going to set the scores right here by analyzing how Pete's right hand changed the world of rock n roll forever. This style could be called ferocious, savage, wild, or all of the above combined.

In this part of this lesson, savage is the keyword. So, you'll learn how to play the guitar with his stamina to make chords thunderous sonic explosions.

Exercise 1

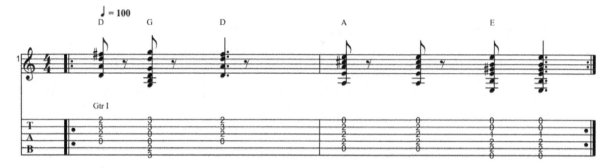

What is paramount to achieving the "Townshend sound" is to hit the guitar as hard as you can in every chord and try to get all notes heard and silence them right before the change of chord.

When you have the dotted figure, do the opposite, and let it ring freely.

Exercise 2

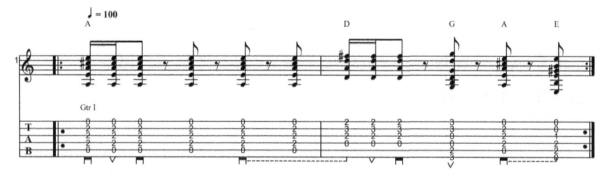

In exercise two, pay close attention to the 16th notes to introduce the chords. This is a trick borrowed by Pete Townshend from flamenco guitar players.

Finally, the guitar player for The Who always plays dreadnaughts and jumbo-style guitars live. Mostly a maple Gibson J-200 and a mahogany Martin D-18.

Spice Up Your Playing: Chords With Passing Lines

In this section, we are going to learn how to add those little passing lines or notes between chords to make your power chords stand out from the crowd.

Well, no, I didn't come up with this technique, it has been a great musical resource for bands the size of Metallica, or The Jimi Hendrix Experience. Indeed, you can find this type of playing in the following songs:

» "Enter Sandman" (Metallica)
» "Hey Joe" (Jimi Hendrix version)
» "Rock n Roll" (Led Zeppelin)
» "Paranoid" (Black Sabbath)
» "Back in Black" (AC-DC)

We are going to see this type of playing using only power chords and a handful of notes from a simple pentatonic scale (which we'll see in the next chapter in all its musical glory).

I Just go where the guitar takes me

- Angus young

Exercise 1

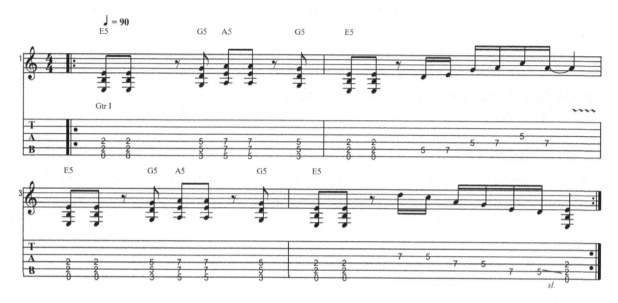

Note in the exercise above how the rests create the syncopation and the passing notes add dynamics to an otherwise 3-power-chord riff.

Speaking of which, this is a great riff to play with a lightweight guitar like an SG or a super strat with humbuckers and a generous amount of distortion.

The Rhythm Master: Keith Richards

Arguably, Keith Richards is the world's most famous rhythm guitar player of all time.

It was bass player Bill Wyman who said that The Rolling Stones are a unique band because unlike every rock n roll band in the world that follows the drummer, the Stones follow the rhythm guitar.

Thus, it is Keith Richards' right hand that's kept the world dancing for over five decades. He can lock in with the band playing parts that make fertile ground for melodies to blossom.

Of course, to achieve this sound you need a mildly overdriven amp (or pedal) and a mighty Fender Telecaster.

Before going to the first exercise, we need to talk about hammer-ons. Keith Richards uses them to "enlarge his chords" making a slight movement that gives dynamics to the music. The idea with hammer-ons is that you play notes without the picking hand, but with the fretting hand only.

In this case, it should happen when strings are ringing from the previous strum.

Exercise 1

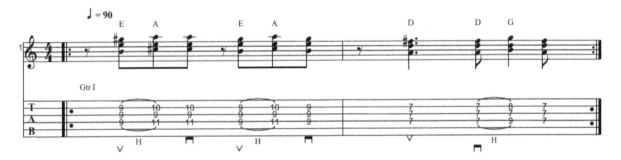

Although you're very familiar with the chord names, we'll use an alternative shape that's way down the neck, close to the 12th fret. These chords give that quintessential "Stones sound" to the playing.

One thing to bear in mind in this exercise, that makes a big difference is to start playing with an upward stroke leaving the silence before strumming. If you ever see Keith Richards playing, you'll see that this movement is part of his stage "dancing".

These are the chords:

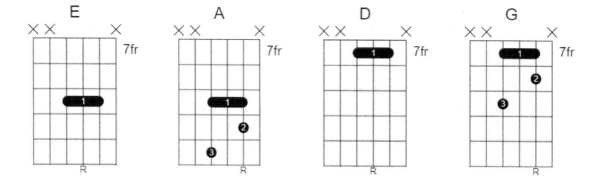

CHAPTER 4

Scales
Building Blocks For Your Solos

Scales are a guitar player's best friend. You can use them to play outrageous solos, beautiful melodies, shred, sing, make thunderous riffs, and make song arrangements. Moreover, you can squeeze all the emotion out of any chord progression if you know what scale to play over it.

That is exactly the reason why we put scales after chords, chord progressions, and rhythm; so you do it in the correct order. Remember the story I told you about my pink hair and Floyd Rose guitar in the first chapters? Well, I did it in the incorrect order and had to relearn everything again to fully understand the power of scales.

Also, and as a final note; practicing scales might be boring, but once you build that muscle memory, you'll become a much better guitar player. Furthermore, if you play the right notes over the right chord in a tight rhythm that locks in with the drummer and bass player, nothing can stop you on your way to world domination.

Without further ado, let's domesticate scales and use them for our benefit.

Go get your favorite shredding-friendly guitar because here we go.

The Root Note In Scales

The root note will determine what key your scale is in. For example, if you take an A minor pentatonic scale, you have its root note as the first thing to play in the 6th string, 5th fret. Then, if you move the same structure two frets up to the 6th string 3rd fret, you have the G Minor Pentatonic Scale.

Scales Have Patterns

Patterns are ways of arranging the notes in a given scale over the fretboard. Just like repeating chords have different "shapes", you can think of the patterns within a scale as the different shapes of the scale on the fretboard.

Understanding Modes

Understanding modes is important to navigate scales easily. These modes are permutations of the parent scale. Although it sounds fancy and difficult, it is as simple as it gets. Let's see the theory through an example that will make everything easier.

For example, let's take the simplest scale: C Major. The C Major scale is, in fact, the Ionian scale and it reads like this:

Ionian: C - D - E - F - G - A - B - C

But what if, instead of starting our scale from C we start it from the second degree (II)? The second degree is obviously D. So if we start the same scale from the second degree, we get the Dorian mode.

Dorian: D - E - F - G - A - B - C - D

Following the same logic, we can create all seven modes by simply moving the first note of our scale. So, the seven modes look something like this:

- » Phrygian: E – F – G – A – B – C – D – E
- » Lydian: F – G – A – B – C – D – E – F
- » Mixolydian: G – A – B – C – D – E – F – G
- » Aeolian: A – B – C – D – E – F – G – A
- » Locrian: B – C – D – E – F – G – A – B

If you want to change the root note of each of these modes to match the piece you're playing on, you need to respect the structure of whole-tone and semitone movements the above notation presents. As long as you respect the intervals, regardless of the root note you choose, each mode will retain its specific tonal qualities.

For example, if you want to play the Aeolian scale over a piece in E, you could transpose it to that root note respecting the intervals and the scale will retain its sad, bittersweet flavor.

Although we won't cover each of the modes, because not all of them are rock n roll compatible, we'll cover the ones you need to know to rip the stage every night.

PRO TIP: Learn the sound of scale rather than plain memorization of the shape. Here's how you do it, play the scale slowly and pay attention to the interval between notes and the tonality. After that, try to contemplate what emotion it is conveying, it could be bright, dark, dreamy, uplifting and so on. This way you can learn any scale by it's sound and not rely solely on the shape. Know that this is extremely useful for writing solos or improvisation.

Minor Pentatonic Scale

The pentatonic scale is called that way because it is made of five notes that repeat in every string. Thus, they generate two types of tonalities: major and minor. Also, it is one of the most used scales in the history of music.

Some examples are:

> » "All Along the Watchtower" (Bob Dylan) The Jimi Hendrix version
> » "Stairway to Heaven" (Led Zeppelin)
> » "Black Dog" (Led Zeppelin)
> » "Rock n Roll" (Led Zeppelin)
> » "Let it be" (The Beatles)

Let's take a look at the first pattern used in the G minor pentatonic scale. Remember that you can play it in the guitar's neck in the two octaves (starting from the 3rd or 15th frets).

The notes in our scale are: G - Bb - C - D - F

The pattern looks like this:

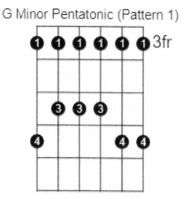

G Minor Pentatonic (Pattern 1)

You'll find the track to hear what it sounds like in our bonus material.

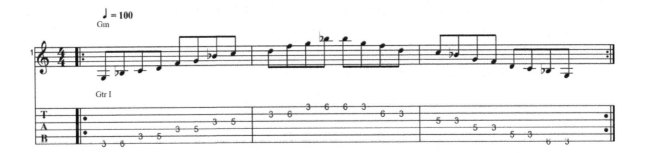

Blues scale

The Blues scale was the first scale I learned how to play and master to follow the steps of my spirit animal: Jimi Hendrix. Although I learned it from him, I found later that it is one of the most used scales in music.

You can hear it in songs like:

- » "Sunshine of your love" (Cream)
- » "Roadhouse Blues" (The Doors)
- » "Enter Sandman" (Metallica)
- » "Heartbreaker" (Led Zeppelin)
- » "Beating around the bush" (AC-DC)

This scale is pentatonic (minor, usually, to get that sad feeling) with an added 6th note. This added note is not just any note, it is "the blue note". Maybe you've heard of the famous place in New York City and the utterly famous record label with the same name. Well, it all comes from the same place: the blues scale.

The blues scale is hexatonic because it has 6 notes instead of 5 as in pentatonic. So, to transform the G minor pentatonic into a blues scale, we need to add the flat V to it. Since the V in the scale of G is D, we have to add a Db to the mix.

Thus, the resulting scale is: G - Bb - C - Db - D - F

This scale works wonders to play melodic lines over minor and 7th chords; of course, you can play the 12-bar blues with it as well.

Let's see what the pattern for this scale looks like:

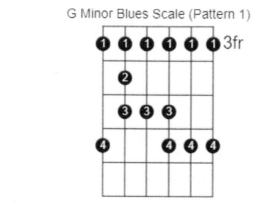

The Dorian Scale

The Dorian scale (you shall also find it as "the Dorian Mode") is the most used diatonic scale for guitar players around the world and can be thought of as an expansion of the minor pentatonic we saw at the beginning of the chapter.

The Dorian scale has 7 notes and contains the entire minor pentatonic, adding two extra notes. This heptatonic scale (because of the 7 notes) sounds unique because it's a "borrowed" resource from jazz.

Some examples of the Dorian scale in action are:

- » Eleanor Rigby (The Beatles)
- » Billie Jean (Michael Jackson)
- » Wicked Game (Chris Isaak)
- » Another Brick in the Wall (Pink Floyd)
- » So What (Miles Davis)

But how do we construct a Dorian scale? Well, we're going to use the same G scale we have been using so far and we need to add two notes: A and E to form a 7-note scale.

As a result, our Dorian G scale looks like this: G - A - Bb - C - D - E - F

We can consider this to be a minor scale due to its flat III (Bb) and flat VII (F) notes. Those are giving our Dorian scale that dark, sad, minor feel.

Let's take a look at what the pattern for the Dorian scale looks like:

G Dorian Scale (Pattern 1)

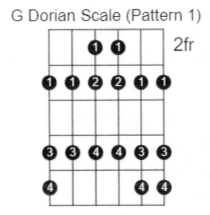

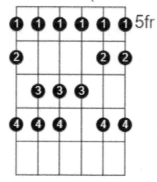

G Dorian Scale (Pattern 2)

The Aeolian Scale

The Aeolian scale is also known as the *natural minor scale* or *relative minor scale* and is a great scale to play over minor and seventh chords. While the Dorian scale has a major sixth, the Aeolian has a minor 6th. That simple detail gives it the perfect sad vibe to play heartbreaking melodies over sad songs.

Some of the songs that made it to the mainstream using the Aeolian scale are:

  » "Smells Like Teen Spirit" (Nirvana)
  » "Dani California" (The Red Hot Chili Peppers)
  » "Not a Second" (The Beatles)
  » "I Was Made for Loving You" (Kiss)
  » "The Trooper" (Iron Maiden)

But how is the Aeolian scale (you can also find it as "Aeolian mode") constructed?

Let's take the same G scale we have been using so far to illustrate the intervals in this scale. Note that you have a minor III and a minor VI.

So, the G Aeolian scale looks like this: G - A - Bb - C - D - Eb - F.

Let's see what do the pattern of this scale looks like on the fretboard:

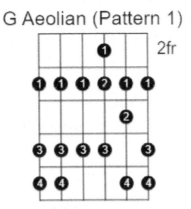

The Mixolydian Scale

I remember the first time I heard "Summer Song" by Joe Satriani. It is a mix of over-the-top playing skills and a melody that's so catchy and festive that I found myself singing it in the shower many times.

With time and practice, I got my chops and was able to pick it up by ear and it was nothing like I had ever played before. I came from minor scales and blues jams and had just started to bend notes to express feelings. Yet, this was something else: it was a song that screamed major chords!

That was how I discovered and fell in love with the Mixolydian scale. It became my go-to scale to spice up the jam nights and try to make people get in a party mood without taking away the feeling in my playing entirely. This is because the Mixolydian scale is close to a major scale but it has a flat VII, making it slightly more obscure and melancholic.

Some of the songs that became worldwide hits utilizing the Mixolydian scale (also known as "mode") are:

- » "Summer Song" (Joe Satriani)
- » "Sweet Home Alabama" (Lynrd Skynyrd)
- » "No Rain" (Blind Melon)
- » "Sweet Child of Mine" (Guns n' Roses)
- » "Third Stone from the Sun" (Jimi Hendrix)

But how is it exactly that you put together a Mixolydian scale to start using it? Well, let's make an example using our beloved G scale again.

The notes in the G Mixolydian scale are: **G - A - B - C - D - E - F**

Remember that the scale features a flat VII that gives it a darker sound and also works wonders over some 12–bar blues progression, 7th chords, and major chords. Let's see what this scale looks like on a guitar fretboard.

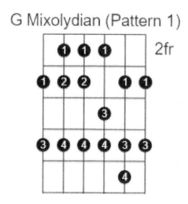

The Major Scale

Speaking of major chords and happy-sounding songs… welcome to the Major Scale! This is a scale that can be used in a plethora of different situations and can help you cheer up whatever you play it on. Furthermore, it is safe to say that the Major scale is the foundation of all Western music.

An insider tip I can give you on this particular scale is that it contains the same notes as an E minor scale. Hence, you can move from one to another seamlessly and always sound in key.

If you are soloing over major chords, the major scale is a match made in heaven.

What are the songs that use the Major Scale? Well, they are far too many for a single book, but here are some examples:

>> "Over the Hills and Far Away" (Led Zeppelin)
>> "Wish You Were Here" (Pink Floyd)
>> "May This Be Love" (Jimi Hendrix)
>> "Nowhere Man" (The Beatles)
>> "Cliffs of Dover" (Eric Johnson)

The notes for the G Major Scale are: **G - A - B - C - D - E - F#**

Let's see what that looks like on the fretboard of our guitars:

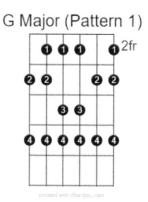

The Harmonic Minor Scale

The Harmonic minor scale is an exotic-sounding scale that can take any chord progression to a new territory. This is because the distance between the VI and VII degrees is one step and a half. This huge leap between the notes is, perhaps, this scale's biggest feature.

Some hit songs made utilizing the Harmonic Minor Scale are:

» "Sweet Dreams" (Eurythmics)
» "Don't Speak" (No Doubt)
» "Smooth" (Santana feat. Rob Thomas)
» "California Dreamin" (Mamas and the Papas)
» "Sultans of Swing" (Dire Straits)

Perhaps, the most recognizable "sadness applied to an upbeat song" tune in the list is "Smooth" (if you are not instantly captivated by Santana's soaring lead guitar on that multi-platinum track, then we have to check your vital signs).

But how do we play the Harmonic Minor Scale on our guitars? Again, we'll use the G scale to illustrate this example.

The notes of the G Harmonic Minor Scale are: G - A - Bb - C - D - Eb - F#

Note how it "jumps" a step and a half from Eb (VI) to F# (VII).

Let's take a look at what this scale looks like on our fretboard:

G Harmonic Minor (Pattern 1)

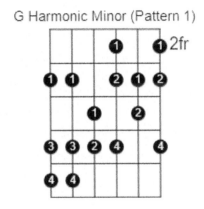

CHAPTER 5

Song Form
Crafting A Song

> You don't just go to the studio and say, 'I'm going to write a hit.' It becomes a hit when people like your compositions.
>
> **- Chuck Berry**

Song Form

At the beginning of this book, I told you all about my endless jamming nights, my pink hair, and my Floyd Rose guitars. I was definitely a man on a mission in my teenage years; I wanted to be the fastest, most rocking guitar player in the world.

Although we could say that time, good advice, and obnoxious amounts of practice made me that kind of a guitar player, I had to endure a similar challenge when I joined my first band. I knew it all about fireworks and playing fast but I didn't have a clue about what it takes to write a song.

It took time, lessons, and patience to write my first decent tunes. That being said, there is no moment more amazing than hearing people chanting and clapping along to a chorus you've come up with.

So, I guess this is another of those "pass it forward" moments of the book in which I share with you all the secrets time and practice have revealed to me.

Go get your guitar and get ready to learn how to make songs because this chapter is all about going from idea to song with a handful of insider tips and just the right amount of theory.

Ready? Here we go!

What Is The Song Form?

We can roughly say that a song form is like a recipe. The song's sections or parts are the steps. These steps are made of different chords and notes which, we could say, are the ingredients. So, mixing the ingredients properly and following the right steps will keep our guests eating with a smile all the way to the dessert.

Some of the most common sections in a song are:

- » Intro
- » Verse
- » Pre-Chorus
- » Chorus
- » Bridge
- » Solo

Although not all of these sections will go into every song, we'll learn each of them and try to make a tune that will reunite them cohesively into a nice-sounding piece.

We'll go through some of the steps you know, like choosing a chord progression, and some you don't know like making a C part modulating to a different key.

Let's take an in-depth look at every section.

Intro

The intro of a song is usually the moment to introduce the elements like rhythm, tempo, feel, key, and instrumentation. As an insider tip, if you happen to sing or work with a singer, it's always better to have the voice decide what key is the most comfortable. We can move up and down the fretboard, but they can't sing out of their reach.

Another important aspect of the intro is that it has to work as an attention-grabber for the listener. Sometimes, those few seconds of the intro are all you have before a random person presses next on Spotify, for example. So, the intro needs to be catchy and cool.

Some great examples of catchy intros could be:

- » "Foxy Lady" (The Jimi Hendrix Experience)
- » "Wish You Were Here" (Pink Floyd)
- » "Are You Gonna Go My Way" (Lenny Kravitz)
- » "Sweet Child of Mine" (Guns n Roses)
- » "We Will Rock You" (Queen)

Although intros are optional, 2 to 4 bars of the intro are very common in popular rock and pop music.

Let's take the key of G major for the first part of our exercise: intro and verse.

The key of G major offers us the following chords: G - Am - Bm - C - D - Em - F#dim

We are going to start on the II degree of our G major scale and follow this progression arpeggiated:

II - IV - V7 - I = Am - C - D7 - G

These are our chords and this is the way we play them:

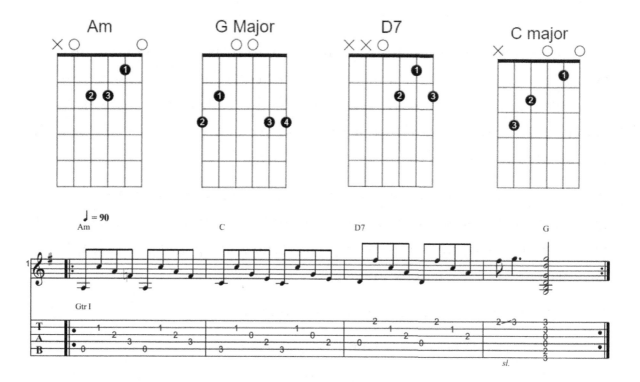

This intro should be played with a clean guitar and a pick. You can add some effects like Delay or Phaser to add a more hypnotic feel to the looping sequence.

> You'll find the track to hear what it sounds like in our bonus material.

Verse

St. Vincent, a great singer-songwriter that has been pushing her (and the world's) music boundaries for decades said once: "verses are yours, choruses are for the audience". What does this mean? Well, it means that sonically and lyrically, your verse will be the "storytelling" part of your song.

So, one thing that I learned the hard way is that we, as guitar players, have to play less to make room for the vocals. Indeed, verses need to work as a fertile ground for the singer's melody to sit comfortably on top.

Hence, in this part of the song, the distortion will kick in but we are going to use palm-muting to keep it under control and save some power for the chorus.

We'll use 3 power chords and one open chord to give it more dynamics. Also, we'll introduce a variation to the D chord called Dsus4.

The chord progression for the verse is:

$$\textbf{VI - IV - I - V = Em - C - G - D}$$

As another insider tip, if you take the VI degree of your scale and use it for the verses, you'll be starting it with a minor chord which makes it a tad more melancholic.

These are the chords and the verse:

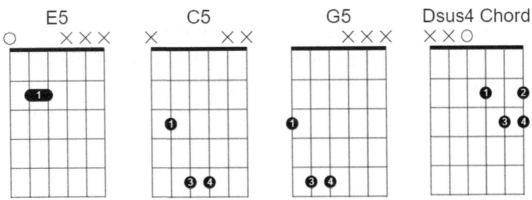

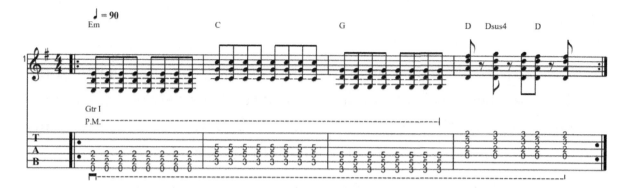

Please note everything is played using downstrokes only and that palm-muting requires distortion, so here is where you step on the pedal.

Pre-Chorus

The pre-chorus is not present in every song but it is a great way to generate tension before releasing it on the chorus. Unlike the verse, the pre-chorus is only a bar or two long. It is also very common to find in this section of songs 7th chords because they are the ultimate tension-risers.

Examples of songs with simple pre-choruses could be "Smells Like Teen Spirit" by Nirvana or "Don't Look Back in Anger" by Oasis.

Here is what this will look like in our song; the chord progression we'll use is different here too.

VI - V - IV - V = Em - D - C - D7

Notice the V degree turned into a 7th chord at the end to take the tension to the maximum and solve it when the chorus kicks in. We'll change the rhythmic pattern too to create an even bigger difference.

These are our chords and pre-chorus:

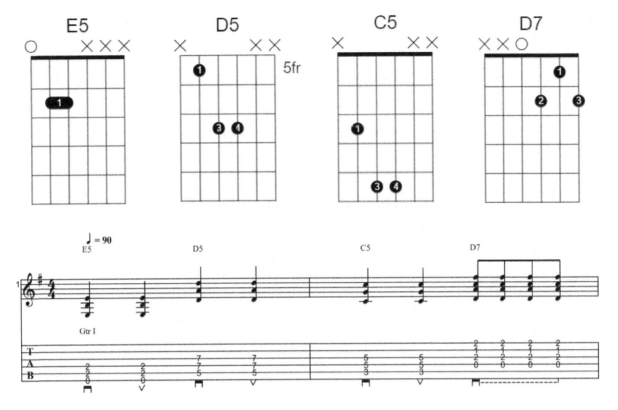

To play it, let the distortion on and try to make the notes last for a full time before playing the next chord. Pay close attention to the picking pattern as it will help you emphasize each part.

Chorus

OK, this is it; the moment we have been building up the tension for: the chorus has arrived. The chorus is not only the most important part of your song, but it can also be the only difference between a hit song and a middle-of-the-chart song.

For our exercise, we are going to go for Oasis-style open big chords that contrast heavily with our arpeggiated intro and our palm-muted verse.

As you play it you're going to feel that the song "takes off" because the chorus starts in the I degree of the scale and uses mostly major chords to convey that feeling of grandiloquence.

Let's take a look at the chord progression, the chords to play, and the chorus itself.

I - V - VI - IV = G - D - Em - C

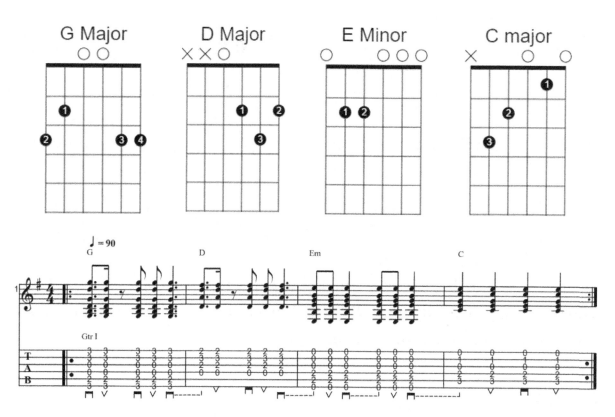

To play this chorus with its open chords it is best to leave the distortion pedal on so it sounds big and full. You can think of it as a big Oasis-like chorus with a minor chord in the middle to keep it emotional and engaging.

To the hell with the rules. If it sounds right, then it is.

- Eddie Van Halen

Bridge

A song's bridge is the songwriter's moment to get a little crazy or experimental. This is because the bridge will very likely only appear once in the entire song while the verse and chorus repeat.

A very cool trick that you can practice on your bridge is modulating to a different, relative key using a pivotal chord that belongs to both keys.

But what is a pivot chord? It is a double agent, a chord that's present in both scales. In this case, the G major chord is the root chord for the G major scale and is also the IV degree in the D major scale.

Hence, we are going to modulate to the D major scale and then find our way back into the chorus.

The D major scale has the following chords:

- » I - D
- » II - Em
- » III - F#m
- » IV - G
- » V - A
- » VI - Bm
- » VII - C# (diminished)

This bridge will happen in the D major scale and we'll modulate back to the chorus through the D major (turning it into a 7th chord since it is also the V degree of the G major scale).

So, let's take a look at our chord progression, chords, and bridge.

IV - III - V - I = G - F#m - A - D

IV - VI - VII - I7 = G - Bm - C# - D7

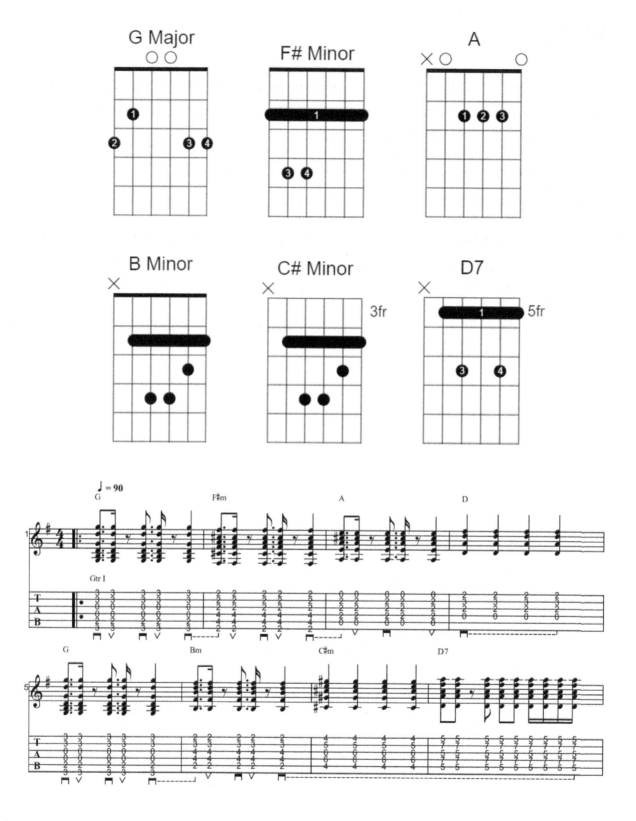

You'll notice that, at the end, the D7 chord begs to go to the I degree of the original scale, which is the G major chord.

Yes, you already know it; it is the first chord of our chorus.

Solo

Not every song features a solo. Yet, wherever there is a solo, it is usually in the key of the song or a relative key.

In this exercise, we are going to play a melodic solo over the verse and a full-on, pyrotechnic solo over the chorus. If you want to, you can join them to create a longer version.

But how do we choose the scale to solo in?

For the first part, we solo over the verse, so I chose the Gm pentatonic because it is great for conveying a little emotion while still playing a rocking scale.

Here's the first part of the solo over the chords of the verse:

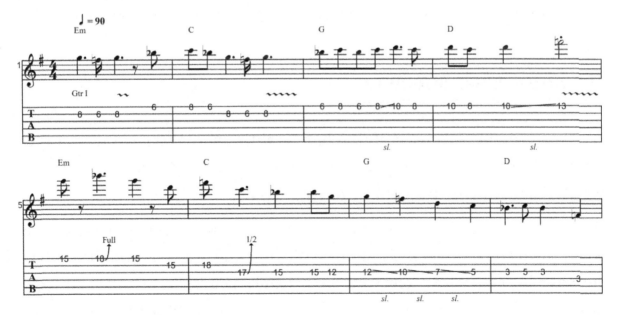

This is a slow-paced solo, with emphasis on melody.

Once you've mastered the solo above, it is time to speed things up.

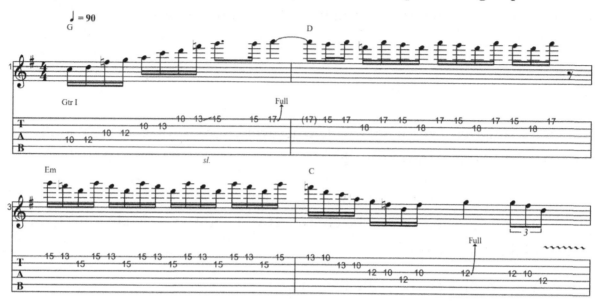

Note how this second solo is not played over the G minor pentatonic but a modulation to the key of D to give it a different flavor. This is the same trick we saw when we saw the bridge section.

Finally, make sure you stick to sixteenth notes with a metronome for the fast parts.

The 12-Bar Blues Structure

Let me begin this final part of the chapter with a tiny little anecdote. I was a little older, the pink hair was gone and I was trying to find my way on a hardtail '79 Stratocaster I found in a pawn shop.

We were jamming some blues and I was trying to push a chord progression when the drummer suddenly stopped playing and stood up from the stool. He was a big man with a long white beard and a ponytail. He looked straight at me and said very clearly: "if you don't know how to play the blues, leave your position to someone else; this is a blues jam."

> **PRO TIP:** Learn the song by understanding it's form, it takes less time to learn the song. Crudely following the lyrics and the chords will only make it harder to memorize a song.

He came and sat next to me after two songs. He apologized first and then said "the blues ain't singing about your broken heart and bending the G string; you gotta master the 12-bar blues, son."

The 12-bar blues doesn't follow a regular song structure; it has a structure of its own.

This is the basic structure:

I - IV - I - I - IV - IV - I - I - V - IV - I - I = G - C - G - G - C - C - G - G - D - C - G - G

Let's divide this structure into four parts.

» Part 1 (bars 1 to 4): I - IV - I - I = G - C - G - G
» Part 2 (bars 2 to 8): IV - IV - I - I = C - C - G - G
» Part 3 (bars 9 to 12): V - IV - I - I = D - C - G - G

You can play it in whatever key you want. For example, the same 12-bar blues structure can be translated to C major and it would look something like this:

» Part 1 (bars 1 to 4): I - IV - I - I = C - F - C - C
» Part 2 (bars 2 to 8): IV - IV - I - I = F - F - C - C
» Part 3 (bars 9 to 12): V - IV - I - I = G - F - C - C

Since degrees I - IV - V are all major in the major keys and minor in the minor keys your chords will always be either all major or all minor so you don't have to worry about that when playing the 12-bar blues.

CHAPTER 6

Technique
Must Know Electric Guitar Technique

Welcome to the second part of the book. Congratulations, you've made it through the fundamentals of rock music and you are ready to hit any stage and do a good job.

Moreover, you're aware of chord progressions and can start writing original material to show the world your feelings and drive crowds insane with your material.

Now, we're heading toward the second part of the book in which I'm going to show you some of my tricks to turn the wonderful into amazing and engage the WOW factor in the audience.

Are you ready to take your playing to the next level?

Go grab your guitar, a hard pick, and buckle up because here we go!

Alternate Picking

Alternate picking can improve your playing immensely. Most likely you'll play effortlessly and sound better too. But don't just take this advice from me, some notable players like Steve Morse (Deep Purple, solo), Yngwie Malmsteen, John McLaughlin, Al Di Meola, Paul Gilbert, and John Petrucci (Dream Theater) based their careers on mastering this technique.

Advantages Of Alternate Picking

Let's see which are the takeaways of mastering this technique:

» Speed - Alternate picking helps you increase your speed.

» Consistency - Once you've mastered alternate picking, your tempo will improve.

» Control - You'll be able to control your picking hand and thus be more accurate.

Down-And-Up Picking

The core of this technique is to use your picking hand alternatively in down and up strokes. This will help your tempo as well because as long as you maintain your picking pattern, you'll always land perfectly on time at the first stroke of each bar.

For this exercise, just use your picking hand and practice alternate picking on a single string.

It looks like this:

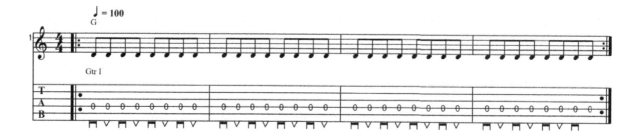

Let me add an insider tip to the exercise, try to use your pick at a 45° angle to the string to avoid it getting stuck between them.

Let's move on to a simple pentatonic scale before we create a riff to play with alternate picking.

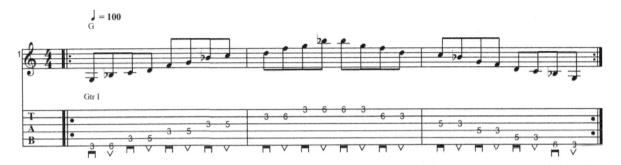

Finally, let's turn this into a small, easy riff so you can practice your newly-acquired skill in the real world in no time. Remember, accuracy is more important than speed.

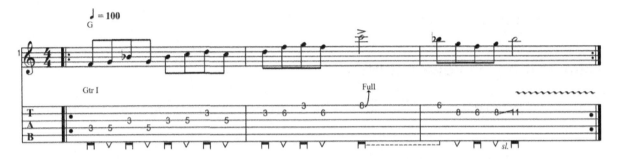

You'll find the track to hear what it sounds like in our bonus material.

Palm-Muting

We've seen a little of what palm-muting is in previous chapters but the time has come to explain this technique in detail and enlarge our scope of action. Here, you'll learn how to use palm-muting on power chords but also when playing solos, riffs, or scales.

If we were to cite songs or bands that serve from this resource to make music, the list would be endless. Therefore, let me give you five examples of songs in which palm-muting is a core element.

- » "Bullets" (Creed)
- » "The Middle" (Jimmy Eat World)
- » "Hash Pipe" (Weezer)
- » "A New Level" (Pantera)
- » "Bored" (Deftones)

Overdrive/Distortion Levels

If you play with overdrive instead of distortion, you have to set your gain post-noon (that's more than 5 if your pedal or amp goes to 10). On the other hand, if you use distortion, you start getting the "chunk" effect at about 3 or 4 if your gain knob goes to 10.

Palm-Muting On Power Chords

The chord progression we'll use will be simple so you can focus on the picking hand.

- » Verse: VI – IV – V - I = F# – D – E - A
- » Pre-chorus: VI - IV - I - V = F# - D - A - E
- » Chorus: I - IV - V - I = A - D - E - A

Our chords will be power chords with an added octave as you've seen before.

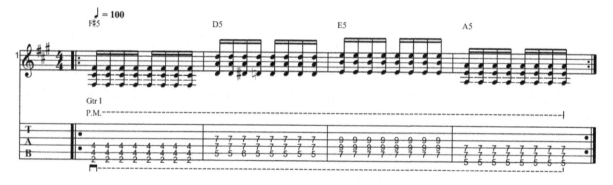

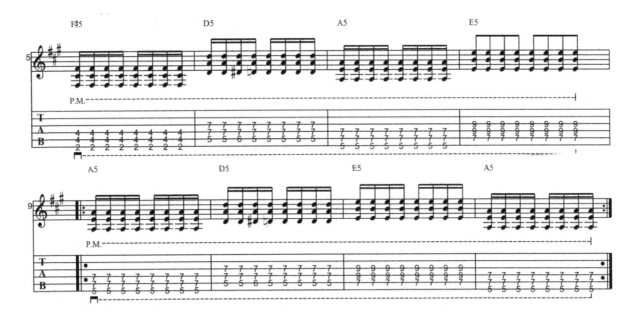

Left And Right-Hand String Muting

You can use muting for more than palm-muting. For example, you can mute the strings when playing chords so only the notes you want are heard.

Left-Hand Muting

To learn to mute unwanted notes, all you have to do is play a C major chord on your guitar including the open sixth string. Now, with the tip of your ring finger try to silence the low E.

It will be hard at first, but once you've mastered this technique, your brain will do it for you 10 times out of 10.

Right-Hand Muting

Sometimes, palm-muting mixed with alternate picking gives the playing a sense of increased speed. Plus, the contrast between the high strings being played with the unmuted pick and the muted low strings is perfect for dynamics.

Let's put this into an exercise so you can learn and use it in your playing.

You'll also notice that I've added many out-of-scale passing notes. These work to create speed and tension, and bring momentum.

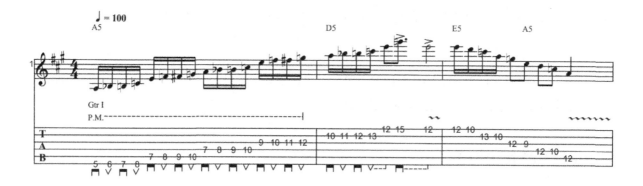

Using Fret Wrap - Advantages & Disadvantages

I'm very sorry to break your heart but guitars are imperfect instruments. Thus, they vibrate in ways we might not want them to.

So, if you want perfect palm-muting sounds, the other strings need to stop vibrating when they are not played. Furthermore, the portion of the strings that is between the nut and the tuners also vibrates.

Let's do a test, grab your guitar and play your low E string strongly. Now touch the rest of the strings; can you feel them vibrate? Repeat the action and check behind the nut, do the strings vibrate?

The Fret Wrap is one of many products to avoid that vibration to make it to the speaker. It can be placed behind the nut to silence the strings not being played.

PROS:

» No loose sounds - You'll only hear what you pick.
» No harmonic overtones - Strings vibrate in frequencies that can excite other strings to get moving and create harmonic overtones that appear as ghost notes in recordings and live performances.

CONS:

» Dead sound - Some players feel that the guitar loses sustain and that open chords tend to fade away sooner.
» No organic sounds due to vibration - Just like vibration on other strings can be bad for tight palm-muting songs, it can be great for open chords and rock n roll rhythm playing.

Legato (hammer-on pull-off)

In this section, I'm going to teach you the technique that players like Joe Satriani, Steve Vai, Allan Holdsworth, Tim Miller, Tom Quayle, and Shawn Lane among many others use to reach MACH 1 on their instruments.

But let me slow down and tell you what this amazing technique is all about.

Hammer-On & Pull-Off

The hammer-on and pull-off techniques are the ingredients of our legato soup. So, exercise 1 is hammer-on. You need to pick the first note only and with a hammer-on (putting your finger down on the note) make the second note ring.

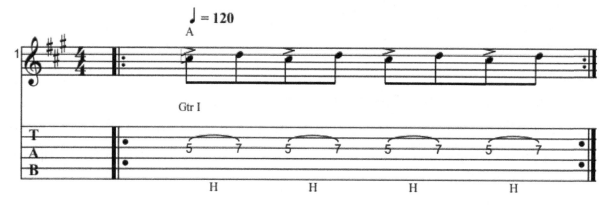

For exercise 2, you're going to have to do the exact opposite as you did before. This time pick the second note (7th fret) and pull it off to make the first note (5th fret) ring without plucking it. That is a pull-off.

> ### Accent
> An accent is an emphasis or stronger attack placed on a particular or set of notes. Often marked as > on the top of the note.

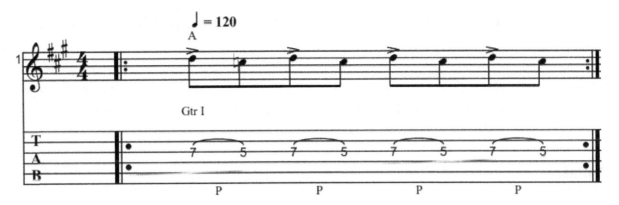

Let's join them in a single exercise so you learn how to mix a hammer-on and a pull-off to make a continuous, smooth sound. Remember that tempo, accuracy, and hearing each note are more important than speed.

Let's play a simple lick using legato. Pay close attention to the picking pattern as well as the legato technique.

As a final piece of advice for this technique; we could call it an insider tip: practice slowly.

Before you know it, your brain is going to go bananas and put legato everywhere which will make you a faster player.

Slide

This technique is not to be confused with "slide guitar" because they are two very different things. This technique is one popularized by guitar virtuosos (maybe we can say, guitar Gods?) Guthrie Govan, Andy Timmons, and Mr. Steve Vai.

The sliding technique demands players to think about scales differently: horizontally. It's also a great way to "break the code" and be more creative in your playing. Once you've pictured the scales that way, you only need to slide your finger through the notes on the scale, plucking only the first one and sliding the rest.

Thus, the sound you get (if the distortion level is correct, AKA everything to 11) will flow as if you were playing with a bow (sorry Jimmy Page, this is the DIY version of your technique).

Exercise 1

Let's spice it up a little and mix it with some of the other techniques you've seen in this chapter.

Exercise 2

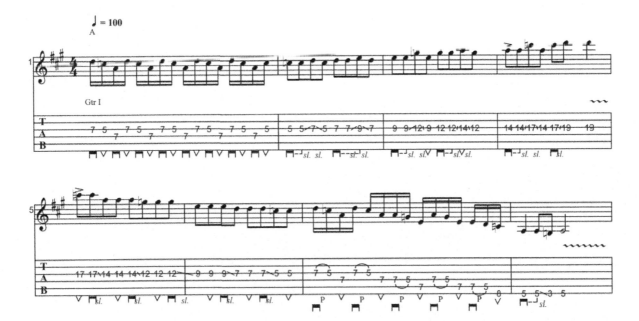

For this exercise, you need to use slide, legato, and play it using alternate picking; three techniques you learned in this chapter.

> Sometimes you want to give up the guitar, you'll hate the guitar. But if you stick with it, you're gonna be rewarded.
>
> **- Jimi Hendrix**

CHAPTER 7

Advanced Technique
More For You

Welcome to the next stage of your guitar playing, we're going to get deep into the most incendiary resources for you to shine on stage.

To begin with, you'll learn the heart and soul of rock guitar soloing which is bending strings to add feeling and emotion to your playing.

Next, we'll go through sweep picking which is a technique that will take your playing to MACH 2.

Finally, one of the most important guitar players of the last 4 decades left us his own legacy. Yes, you'll learn tapping in the style of Eddie Van Halen.

So, are you ready to take your guitar playing to the ultimate level?

Go get your guitar because here we go!

Bending

Bending is, perhaps, the most widely used resource for guitar players in the world. Players like the great Brian May, Carlos, Jimi, the three kings (BB, Albert, and Freddy), Stevie Ray Vaughan, David Gilmour, and Eric Clapton among countless others.

It is also the most emotionally expressive technique on the guitar. I remember the first time it happened to me. I had just had my heart broken for the first time and I was a complete emotional mess. It was a 12-bar blues in A and I bent the G string and the moaning sound of my guitar somehow aligned with my broken heart and I felt the connection.

From that moment on, the guitar became an outlet to express my deepest feelings and a lifelong companion. It is time for me to pass that teaching to you and hopefully inspire you to connect to the instrument the same way I did. You'll never feel alone again.

The Basics Of Bending

What does it mean to bend a string? Well, the idea is to make one note sound like another, higher note. For example, if you bend your G string at the 7th fret up a whole tone you can transform that D into an E.

Let's see the most common variations of the bending technique in the shape of some exercises.

Whole Tone Bend

When bending a whole tone, you are taking the original note up two semitones, AKA, two frets.

Let's see how it's done in an exercise:

Semitone Bend

When bending a semitone, we're moving from one note to the next fret.

Let's see how it's done in an exercise:

Bend & Release

This is a great technique that can make your playing get seriously emotional. You have to take your time bending the note, reaching the next note (semitone, whole tone), and letting it go back to the original.

You can hear it all over any of the blues players we cited above, especially when they are going for a melodic line.

Let's take a look at this trick in an exercise:

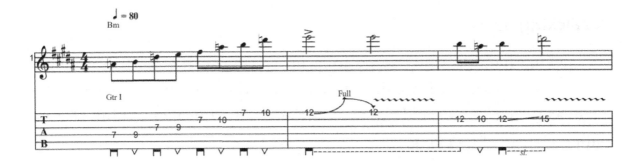

Pre-Bend

The main idea of a prebend is to pluck the note when it's already bent and let it come down to the original pitch.

Let's see what that sounds like in the shape of an exercise:

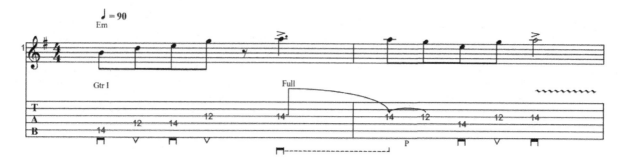

Sweep Picking

This technique will speed up your playing from the speed of sound to the speed of light. It was mastered by guitar geniuses such as Yngwie Malmsteen, Frank Gambale, and Jason Becker among others.

Let's divide the explanation into two: the picking hand and the fretting hand.

The Picking Hand

The picking hand is going to go from one string to the next in a single movement as if the pick would fall down. On the way up, the idea is the same, as if your hand could fall up effortlessly. Furthermore, think of it as gliding instead of plucking.

Also, with the palm of your hand, you have to immediately palm-mute the string you've just played so it won't ring more than needed.

The Fretting Hand

For this technique, the fretting hand needs to lift every finger immediately after playing each note so they won't ring more than needed.

Moreover, it is paramount to use a fretting-hand muting technique (as you've seen before in this book) to avoid the unnecessary ringing of the notes.

Exercising

This is a technique that pros use to reach insane tempos. For example, you can check Cacophony's (Marty Friedman and Jason Becker's band) album called "Speed Metal Symphony" and hear some extreme sweep picking at lightning-speed tempos.

We'll set the tempo at 100 so you can build up your speed slowly. Let me give you two insider tips:

» Focus on the metronome - While trying to go faster, it is common to go off-tempo so, practice with a metronome and go slow.
» Mind the ringing strings - Speed without control is useless. So, make sure that you pay attention to the muting part with both hands. If you can, record yourself doing it.

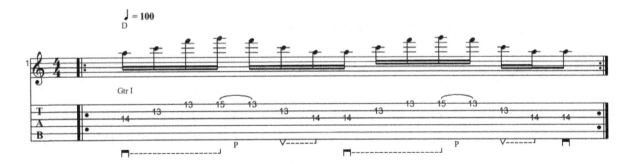

Tapping

Although I was too young to have seen Eddie Van Halen rip the stage of the '83 US Festival showing the world we had misunderstood and understated what a guitar can do, I was a pre-teen in 1995. Seeing him play that long Eruption solo in Toronto with the purple bandana on his head changed me forever. I couldn't tell if the smoke was coming from the cigarette or the fretboard!

Uncle Ed was the ultimate fireworks guitar player and he changed guitar playing forever.

For example, if you hear Joe Satriani's *Midnight* or Steve Vai's *Building the Church* you can see tapping at speeds and in shapes unheard of.

Still, the inspiration for them was Eddie Van Halen.

Why Learn Tapping?

Tapping is, we could say, the ace up your sleeve. To begin with, those who aren't guitar players will be fascinated by it and think you're some kind of alien with a guitar doing impossible things. On the other hand, fellow guitar players will enjoy that you are bringing more resources to the fretboard to create different sonic landscapes.

In a nutshell, tapping is always a killer on stage.

The Basic Idea

You've seen in the last chapter that hammer-ons and pull-offs are a great way to speed up your playing. Well, the idea of tapping is to add the picking hand as another hammer-on/pull-off element to the mix.

So, your fretting hand will be doing something similar to what you learned in the previous chapter but the picking hand will be hammering on and pulling off too.

For example, let's use the A Minor pentatonic. The first thing you need to do is to place your index finger on the 5th fret of the 1st string and your little finger at the 8th fret.

Now, remove the little finger while leaving your index on the 5th fret. With your picking hand, use either the index or the middle finger to tap on the 12th fret at the first string. That tapping works as a hammer-on and needs to be followed by a pull-off with the same finger.

As you pull off the string on the 12th fret, the note you've fretted on your index finger will ring. Finally, you need to hammer on with your little finger on the 8th fret.

A good piece of advice is to set your guitar's volume at 0 (if it's electric and it's plugged into roaring levels of distortion) and try to make it sound loud and clear unplugged.

Eddie did this and then moved both his hands to follow the notes needed in the scale he was playing on, and that is what we are going to do too. This needs to be done in either 8th notes or 16th notes triplets.

Let's see what this exercise looks like:

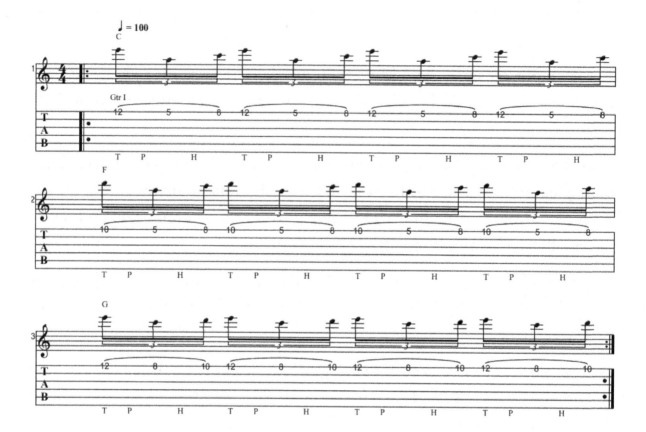

CHAPTER 8

Licks
Steal From Masters

This is it, the final lesson. Here, we will combine everything you learned so far in a single chapter. Plus, you'll learn licks that will help you sound closer to some of the greatest guitar players of all time.

The idea is that the tricks that made them worldwide famous can nourish your playing and, somehow, become your own.

Therefore, learn all the 14 licks in this chapter and then tweak them to make them more comfortable: more you.

Go grab your guitar, there's a lot of playing coming and it's going to be a blast.

SRV- Style Lick

Stevie Ray Vaughan left us too soon but his playing will live forever. He was a new definition of emotion mixed with skill and power.

Despite having an infinite assortment of techniques to choose from, his open-position playing was beyond anyone else's. He would use the open position of the E scale and create unique compositions that sounded like nobody but him.

That's exactly what we're about to learn.

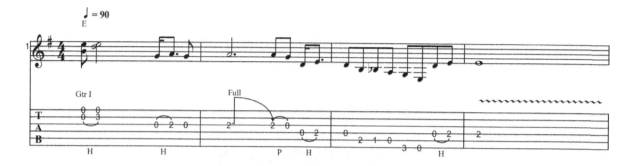

Eric Clapton- Style Lick

Few players like Eric Clapton can afford to aim for feel and emotion instead of speed. You have to be THAT good.

The next exercise is in the A aeolian scale which adds some notes that give it a more intense vibe and scream slow blues in all directions. So, the whole idea of learning this lick is playing slow and melodically to bring people into your music.

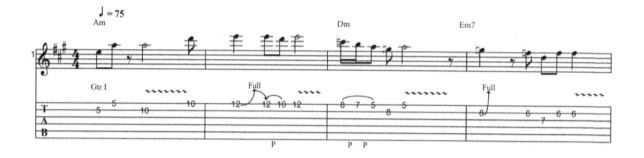

Jimi Hendrix- Style Lick

Jimi Hendrix is, without the shadow of a doubt, my biggest influence of all time. No other guitar player blew my mind rhythmically, harmonically, technically, or emotionally as he did.

Although he was, in my opinion, the wildest guitar player to ever set foot on this Earth, I love his melodic playing the most. He was one of the guitar players that best embodied the double-stops (playing two strings together at the same time). He added hammer-ons to make it sound… well, like himself.

This next exercise is full of that and is played in the E minor pentatonic all across the fretboard just like he did.

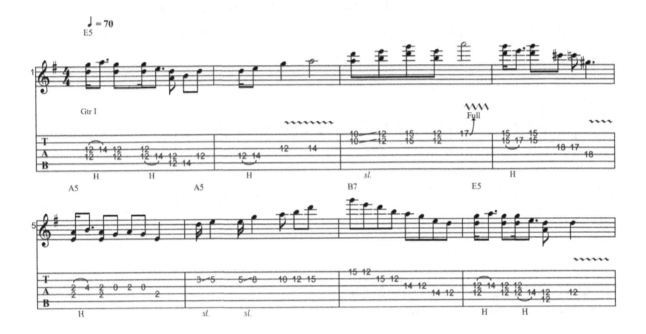

> I believe every guitar player inherently has something unique about their playing. They just have to identify what makes them different and develop it.
>
> **- Jimmy Page**

Duane Allman- Style Lick

Passing away at only 24 years old didn't stop Duane Allman from becoming one of the most revered guitar players in the history of music. He was one of the best slide guitar players of his generation and very well-known for being a master at improvising using Mixolydian scales and triplets.

In this exercise, we're going to use the D Mixolydian scale to create an Allman-inspired lick that will help you play fast and fun licks utilizing minimum finger movements.

Ritchie Blackmore- Style Lick

Ritchie Blackmoore is one of the most influential guitar players in the history of music. First, as one of the founding members and lead guitarist of Deep Purple, then as the founder and main axman of Rainbow.

Bear in mind the lick contains half notes (bent with vibrato) with sixteenth notes played super fast. He did that to add dynamics to the E harmonic minor scale.

Have fun!

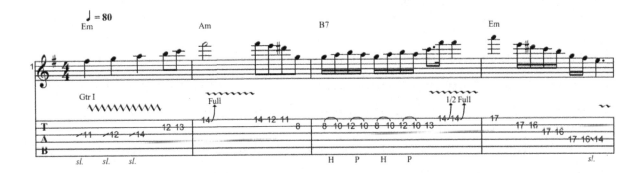

David Gilmour- Style Lick

David Gilmour is, perhaps, the most lucid melodic guitar player of his generation. Moreover, as part of Pink Floyd, one of the most important progressive, conceptual bands in the history of music he created the kind of solos you can sing as if it was lyrics.

In this lick, we'll explore his style with an A minor pentatonic. David bends the same note a half step and then a whole step a lot as you'll find here.

Have fun!

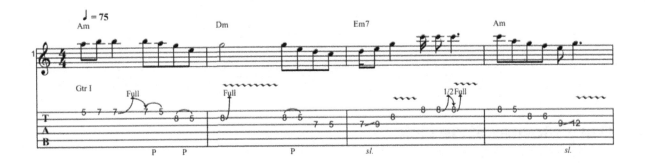

Jimmy Page- Style Lick

Jimmy Page is one of those guitar players that don't need any introduction at all. He was Led Zeppelin's only guitar player and the person responsible for some of the most iconic and complex riffs in the history of rock n roll.

One of his main skills was being ferocious on stage with repeating licks that would take the entire band to the verge of exploding all the time.

Pay special attention to the section where the third string gets bent while the second string remains on pitch.

Have fun!

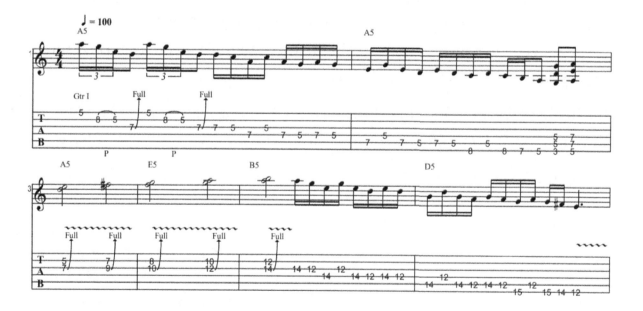

Gary Moore- Style Lick

Few times in my life have I heard anyone bend strings like Gary Moore did. He used to bend them a whole step and a half playing over the legendary II - V - I - IV chord progression and using a harmonic minor scale.

So, this lick will teach you to mix half notes with lightning-fast sixteenth notes and a bend that goes a whole step and half more.

Have fun!

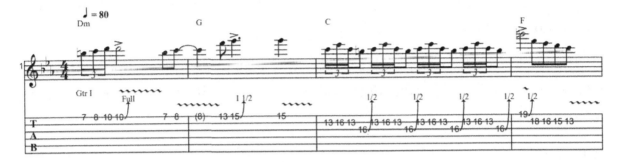

Brain May- Style Lick

Besides being the creator of some of the most important arena anthems of the '80s next to the late and grandiose Freddy Mercury, Brian May is also a guitar player so unique that he could never be replaced or imitated.

This lick features some very strong bends mixed with hammer-on and pull-offs with some of the extra notes that the Aeolian scale offers to add sugar to the mix.

Finally, add the necessary distortion and delay to the tone of your guitar; close your eyes and hear Wembley sing every note with you.

Have fun!

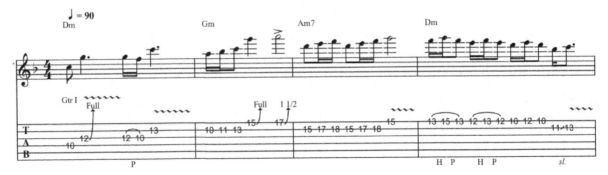

Carlos Santana- Style Lick

If Jimi Hendrix is my biggest influence, Santana definitely takes the second spot on that podium. Indeed, there are very few players that can play a single note and let us know it's them.

In this lick, you'll notice some rests and repeated notes. It's something Carlos used to do in the Woodstock days. Also, you'll notice some repeating legato notes.

Have fun!

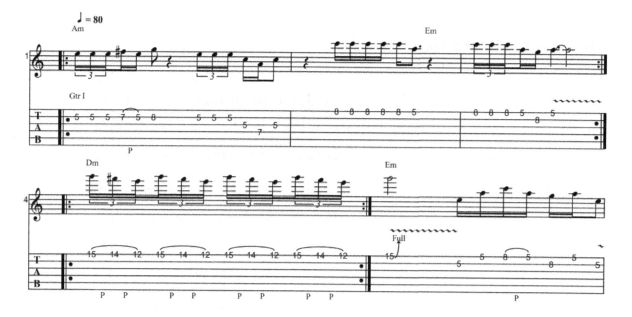

Steve Morse- Style Lick

Steve Morse is one of those players who need no introduction.

Not only did he step up to the challenge of filling Ritchie Blackmoore's shoes as the main guitar player for Deep Purple, but he is also a prolific player with a plethora of projects in which quality, speed, and accuracy ooze from his fingers.

In this lick, we'll use the minor E pentatonic with some cool chromatic notes added.

Have fun!

Eddie Van Halen- Style Lick

Eddie Van Halen changed guitar playing forever.

In this exercise, we are going to take a look at one of Edward's most celebrated techniques: tapping. Moreover, it's mixed with palm muting and alternate picking to triple the fun.

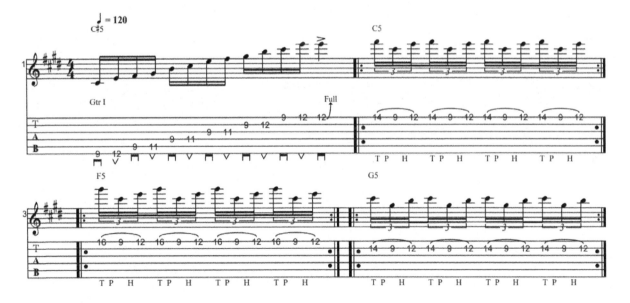

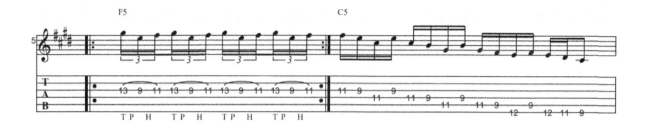

Joe Satriani- Style Lick

What Eddie did with his tapping technique, Joe did with his legato technique.

As an insider tip, don't overlook the fact that these are sixteenth notes triplets. Practice them slowly, one at a time until you master the idea, and only then speed it up.

Have Satch-approved fun!

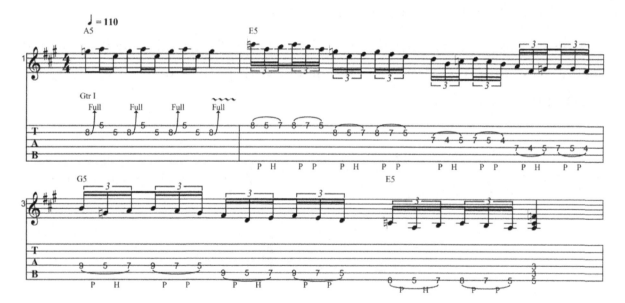

Slash- Style Lick

I told you about hearing the riff from "Sweet Child o' Mine" more than any other thing in my life at the time I sold guitars. It is not a coincidence, it is the result of creating guitar lines that have an almost vocal quality and that are also fast, rocking, and scorching-hot.

Thus, in this exercise, you'll learn how to bend the strings the way Slash does in a repeated ascending sequence and also how to do hammer-ons, pull-offs, and slides in a descending way just like he does.

Enjoy!

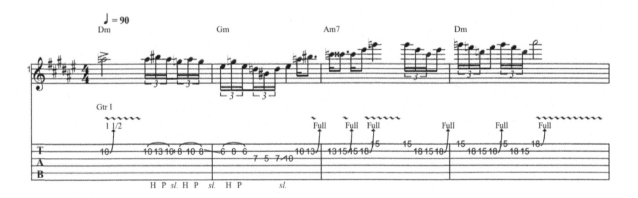

CHAPTER 9

Gear
Where to Invest Money

 Your sound is in your hands as much as anything. It's the way you pick, and the way you hold the guitar, more than it is the amp or the guitar you use.

- **Stevie Ray Vaughan**

As someone who has collected guitars, amps, and effect boxes (especially effect boxes) for most of his life, I have to tell you that gear does make a difference. Certain frequencies ring stronger, sound clearer, and are more musical, and that makes music more pleasing to the ear of the player and the listener.

Moreover, effect boxes can work as an inspiration and can help you paint on your canvas with more colors expanding your sonic horizons (sk Mr. The Edge how important effects are for modern music).

So, we are going to go deep into the best-known kinds of guitars, amps, effects, and software so you can make informed decisions about what to buy and why.

Get ready to start planning your collection because here we go, it's gear time!

Guitar

The Fender Stratocaster

The Stratocaster was introduced to the world in 1954 as a top-of-the-line model that was to bring the brand finally to the mainstream. Leo Fender was an electronic engineer rather than a musician. So, he was after the perfect guitar design.

Not only did he succeed at it, but the Stratocaster has largely been unmodified until this day, almost 70 years later. Moreover, the Fender Stratocaster is the best-selling guitar of all time.

Thus, the sound and looks of the Stratocaster became a part of so many iconic recordings that nowadays it is impossible to take them out of our collective memory or ears.

So, if you want to be a lead guitar player and get the piercing blues-rock sounds of players like Jeff Beck, Ritchie Blackmoore, or Jimi Hendrix, Strat's the way.

Main Specs:

» Body - Alder or ash with contoured edges.

» Neck - Bolt-on maple.

» Fretboard - In the '50s maple only; rosewood available since 1960.

» Electronics - 3 single-coil pickups, 2 tone knobs, 1 volume knob, and a 5-way switch.

» Tremolo system - Hardtail or Fender's vibrato system.

The Fender Telecaster

Although the Stratocaster is Fender's most famous creation, the Telecaster started the legend in 1952.

This guitar is what most people know as a workhorse. It is a two-pickup, two-knob configuration and it has been the guitar of choice for rhythmic guitar players for decades. Indeed, just like Jimi Hendrix cut through the very fabric of music with a Stratocaster, Keith Richards, Bruce Springsteen, Andy Summers, and Joe Strummer among many others played rhythm guitar on their teles.

Main Specs:

- » Body - Alder or ash.
- » Neck - Bolt-on maple.
- » Fretboard - In the '50s only maple, rosewood is a choice since 1960.
- » Electronics - 2 single-coil pickups, 1 tone knob, 1 volume knob, and a 3-way switch.
- » Tremolo system - Hardtail with string-through-body design for added sustain.

The Gibson Les Paul

Although most people don't know this, the Gibson Les Paul is a signature model. Indeed, Les Paul was a virtuoso jazz guitar player that lived to be 94 years old and remained active musically through much of his time.

The Gibson Les Paul model was first introduced to the world in 1952. Its first iteration was not like the one we know today; it featured a stop tailpiece and dual P-90 pickups (single-coils on steroids). In fact, it didn't feature humbuckers until 1957 and was only offered in gold top finish until 1958 when sunburst (a finish offered only in higher-end jazz models) became available.

Names like Joe Perry, Jimmy Page, Gary Moore, Slash, Billy Gibbons, and Mark Knopfler feed this guitar's legendary status in rock n roll.

This is because the Les Paul is a very rocking guitar with its low end coming from the mahogany body and neck, the singing highs from the maple top, and the screaming humbuckers.

For those about to rock, trying out a Les Paul is a must.

Main Specs:

- » Body - Mahogany with a maple top.
- » Neck - Mahogany set-neck.

- » Fretboard - Rosewood, ebony for the Les Paul Custom models
- » Electronics - 2 Humbucker pickups, 2 tone knobs, 2 volume knobs, 3-way switch.
- » Tremolo system - Gibson tune-o-matic.

The Gibson ES-335

The Gibson ES-335 is the world's first semi-hollow electric guitar ever released to the market. The big difference between the ES-335 and its predecessors is that the guitar features a center maple block with hollow sides. Therefore, it can be played at a much higher volume without fighting with feedback.

The configuration is similar to that of the Les Paul, with 2 humbucking pickups, four knobs, and a 3-way switch. That being said, the ES-335 was the favorite of rock and roll pioneers because it could drive an amp easier into distortion because of the body being half hollow.

If you want to create the wall of sound with open chords Oasis became famous for, infinite sustain like BB King, or soaring rocking tones like Dave Grohl, an ES-335 is the way.

Main Specs:

- » Body - 3-ply maple/poplar/maple with a maple center block.
- » Neck - Mahogany.
- » Fretboard - Rosewood.
- » Electronics - 2 humbucker pickups, 2 tone knobs, 2 volume knobs, 3-way switch.
- » Tremolo system - Gibson tune-o-matic. Only some models feature a Bigsby tremolo.

The Super Strats

The Fender Stratocaster is not only the best-selling guitar of all time, but it is also the one that inspired many. The metal, hard rock, and thrash embraced this shape and did some serious overhauling to make it an '80s-friendly instrument.

Indeed, brands like Charvel, Jackson, Ibanez, ESP, Kramer, and Schecter among others added Floyd Rose tremolos, active humbuckers, and simplified controls to turn strats into metal machines.

If you want to sound like Kirk Hammett, Joe Satriani, Steve Vai, Richie Sambora, or Eddie Van Halen, shredding on an ultra-thin neck with tons of distortion, Super Strats are the way to go.

Main Specs:

» Body - Alder, ash, or basswood.

» Neck - Maple.

» Fretboard - Maple usually sounds more fierce with distortion, rosewood adds a tad of sweetness to the sound.

» Electronics - 1, 2, or 3 humbuckers, 1 tone knob, 1 volume knob, 3 or 5-way switch. It is possible to find single-coil configurations too like HSH or HSS.

» Tremolo system - Most superstrats feature Floyd Rose tremolos. It is also possible to find them in hardtail, stop tailpiece, or regular tremolo configurations too.

Amplifiers

Let's Talk Marshalls and Rock

The first amplifier brand that comes to mind when talking about rock is Marshall. This British brand has been the main driving force for rockers for over six decades. It was created by a drummer named Jim Marshall in 1962.

The amps Jim made performed perfectly for the growing rock n roll scene in the '60s.

The seventies and eighties saw rockers embrace Marshall and vice versa with epic models such as the JMP and JCM800. By the 90s, players like Dave Navarro based their tone on the JCM900. In the 2000s, players like Joe Satriani took the new 3-channel JCM2000s around the world.

Nowadays, Marshall is the "brown sound" behind legends like AC-DC, Slash, Red Hot Chili Peppers, Aerosmith, Led Zeppelin, Oasis, Ozzy Osborne, and many more.

What About Vox Amplification?

Three examples define the history of Vox Amplification: The Beatles, Queen, and U2. Indeed, these three acts swear by their Vox amps and don't use anything else. For example, Brian May tours with 12 Vox combos to get his signature sound.

Although both brands were born in 1962, the big difference between Vox and Marshall is in the valve the companies used. While Marshall focused on big sounds coming from 25-watt EL34s, Vox used 12.5-watts EL84s. This slight difference became the reason why some players preferred one brand or the other. Also, the AC-15 and AC-30 are combo amplifiers that have a Fender vibe adding reverb and tremolo as standard features.

The Fender Deluxe Reverb, The Hidden Gem

While in England in the '60s it was all about big distorted sounds and rock n roll, back in the USA, Fender was trying to refine its amplifiers to get the ultimate clean sound with reverb and tremolo.

The brand had introduced the Twin Reverb (a big amplifier with 2x12" speakers) in 1952. These tweed Twin Reverb amps can still be seen on stage whenever The Rolling Stones play to this day.

Still, Fender perfected the design even further and in 1963 the Fender Deluxe Reverb was born.

This amp, a 22-watt, single 12" speaker iteration of its bigger brother, became Fender's most sought-after amplifier. This is because you can set the volume at 5 in any small venue and get mildly overdriven tones with tube-driven reverb and tremolo.

So, if you're after the tones of players like Johnny Marr, Stevie Ray Vaughan, John Mayer, Mac Demarco, and Kevin Parker, this amp is the hidden gem that can change your tone.

Hiwatt Amplification, The Unsung Heroes Of Rock N Roll

Although most people think that Marshall is the definitive British rock sound, Hiwatt is the brand connoisseurs around the world tend to gravitate to.

Hiwatt amplification sounds nothing like Marshall, Vox, or Fender; it has a sound of its own. Hiwatts sound not only brighter but also heavier. They make amazing blues amps when clean and incredible rock amps when pushed.

For example, The Who's "We won't get fooled again" is a great example of how the soaring tones don't have opaque or mid-infused sounds but remain bright and huge.

Pedals

The Never-Ending Story Of The Perfect Overdrive Pedal

Overdrive pedals are not to be confused with distortion pedals. While these emulate the natural sound of a pushed amp, distortion is an effect that alters your tone.

Let's talk about the most important two.

The Tube Screamer

The Tube Screamer (TS9, TS808, TS10), created by Ibanez in 1979, is one of the most famous overdrive pedals of all time. It is very intense on the midrange and utilizes only three controls: drive, tone, and level.

Guitar players like Stevie Ray Vaughan, Mark Knopfler, Gary Moore, Joe Bonamassa, and John Mayer base most of their tone on it.

The Boss Blues Driver

Those who don't like Tube Screamers for being too *midrangey*, swear by this pedal, created by Boss in 1995 because it adds no to the signal, just a mild overdrive.

Therefore, players who don't take the blues as their main canvas to paint their souls like Kevin Parker, Tom Morello, Billie Joe Armstrong, Prince, or Robert Smith play through this pedal.

Distortion & Fuzz

While overdrive is subtle and doesn't change your tone but adds color to it, distortion is the complete opposite, it changes your tone and adds other qualities to it. Furthermore, if we were to make a scale from subtle to extreme, we could place overdrive, distortion, and fuzz as three rising levels.

Distortion became very popular, especially in the '80s and '90s when players were looking for angry tones with lots of clarity and a very tight low end.

For example, the Boss DS-2 Turbo on John Frusciante's distorted part in "Danny California".

Fuzz, on the other hand, sounds more like a sound explosion taking any tone to the extreme. Perhaps, the most famous example is Jack White during his White Stripes era in which all he had was an Electro Harmonix Big Muff.

Can overdrive, distortion, and fuzz pedals co-exist? Moreover, can they be used combined? The answer to both questions is yes.

Opening The Scope, A Short Guide On Modulation Pedals

Modulation pedals are the perfect way to enlarge your sonic landscape and make your guitar a texture-rich instrument.

Let's go through the four most important ones you should know about.

Chorus

The original Boss CE-1 dates back to 1976. The idea of this pedal is that the guitar sound is copied and repeated at a different, very close time with a modulated pitch. Thus, the effect adds motion, dynamics, and texture to any sound.

It was one of the very few pedals that Nirvana's frontman Kurt Cobain ever used. The intro to "Come as you are" is a great example of it.

Famous models: Boss CE-2, Electro Harmonix Small Clone, and TC Electronics Corona.

Phaser

The phaser is made by dividing the signal into two and altering the phase of one of them. This creates a swirling effect.

For example, it was Eddie Van Halen's secret to his dynamic-filled lead playing. Also, songs like "Breath" by Pink Floyd or "Ten Years Gone" by Led Zeppelin feature this effect.

Famous models: MXR Phase 90, Electro Harmonix Small Stone, and DOD Phasor 201.

Flanger

If we were to order these pedals for their level of sound alteration, the chorus is the most subtle, phaser takes things a little further, and flanger is the '80s version of that.

Flanger adds another guitar line with a slight delay (usually less than 20 milliseconds) which creates a comb filter effect.

Some songs to appreciate this effect can be "Barracuda" by Heart, "Life in the fast lane" by The Eagles, and "Head over heels" by Tears for Fears.

Famous models: Electric Harmonix Electric Mistress, Boss BF-3, and MXR Flanger.

Uni-vibe

The Uni-Vibe emulates the sound of a Leslie Rotary Speaker. This device is a speaker inside a box with a rotating motor that could create a sweeping effect that psychedelic bands embraced. A good example of its sound is The Beatles' "Tomorrow Never Knows", or "Little Wing" by Jimi Hendrix.

Famous models: Jim Dunlop Uni-Vibe, Fulltone Deja-Vibe, and UniVox Uni-Vibe.

Did Anyone Say Delay -Ay -Ay -Ay?

Perhaps, the dealy is the most widely used guitar pedal of all time.

The idea of the effect is very simple, it samples the original sound and repeats it with a delay from the original.

There is no other player that used this effect more iconically than U2's The Edge. You can hear it all over the band's early records; for example, in songs like "Where the streets have no name" or "Pride (in the name of love)".

Also, guitar players trying to thicken up their lead sound usually turn on the delay for solos like Steve Vai, Joe Satriani, and David Gilmour.

Famous models: Electro Harmonix Memory Man, Boss DD3 Digital Delay, and MXR Carbon Copy.

Reverb Is The New (Old) Thing

Reverb is an effect that is naturally created by the bouncing of the audio signals when in a closed space. For example, if you walk into an empty church and speak out loud, you'll find that your voice reverberates.

Fender amplifiers emulated this sound with spring tanks and valves. Although it had faded away in the '80s and '90s, it made a stellar comeback in the last couple of decades. You can hear it on bands like Warpaint, or My Bloody Valentine.

Famous pedals: Strymon Blue Sky, TC Electronics Hall of Fame, and Boss RE-2 Space Echo.

The All-In-One Multi-FX Solutions

I know what you're thinking while you scratch the top of your head with your index finger: "man, that's a lot of pedals and a lot of money!" Well, worry not because some of the most famous effects brands in the world thought this before us and created what we know as multi-fx processors.

These floor-based creations hold all the effects above in the same box for a fraction of the price the combination of them would cost. Thus, they are the perfect way to get started until you know what effects go with you, your music, your playing style, and your personality.

I started that way, I bought a Boss ME-30 when I was 16 and it taught me everything.

Moreover, modern ones can be plugged directly into the speakers, or to a computer.

Moreover, brands like Kemper, Headrush, Fractal, and Line6 created solutions that can be heard on some of the biggest stages in the world.

So, from inexpensive bedroom practice to headlining Glastonbury, multi-fx processors can take your playing to new places and are great to have a taste of what you like and what you don't.

What Is The VST Hype All About?

Computers are becoming more of an integral part of musicians' lives by the day.

VST (Virtual Studio Equipment) is the next level of music-oriented software. For example, IK Multimedia created Amplitube in 2002. A couple of decades later, it

is so real even an old wolf like me (who has a Deluxe Reverb and a couple of original Tube Screamers) chooses to go straight into the computer to make demos and casual recordings.

We could have the same conversation that a Spotify user can have with a record collector. The real thing sounds like the real thing, but the possibilities and comfort of VST are uncanny.

Finally, VSTs can be integrated with your favorite DAW so you can record your guitar straight into the computer anytime anywhere.

If you think VST is a hype, check again, it is a powerful, handy tool.

Conclusion

We started this book with a promise, to make you a better player.

Our definition of a "better player" is a complete, and technically-advanced player.

A player that can hear and understand music and that can make discerning, informed decisions taking songs and compositions to a pro-level. Also, a player that understands the rhythmic nature of our instrument. Finally, a player who can get on a stage and leave an entire venue in awe with tricks, melodies, and pyrotechnics.

The end of your journey as a reader is the beginning of a new stage in your journey as a player.

Go out there, show them what you've learned, and may the rest be rock n roll history in the making.

Thank You Note

Thank you so much for allowing me to guide you on this endless and beautiful path, guitar playing is. I had a blast writing this book for you and I hope I inspired and made you laugh a bit with my old-man stories. But above that, I hope that you too had a blast learning new techniques and playing like the best guitar players of all time.

The road to stardom is made of patience, hard work, the right amount of musical theory, and the right advice; hopefully, this book covers 2 out of 4.

I wish you the best of luck and may guitar playing be your companion and best friend for a lifetime.

Farewell

Pssssttt....

What are you doing here? Are you lost?

Do people even look at the last pages of a book?

Jokes aside, If you enjoyed this book, could you take 2 minutes to leave a review about it?

Reviews are the lifeblood for small publishers and help us get our books into the hands of more guitarists like you.

We read every review personally and appreciate each one of it.

To leave a review, simply go to the platform you purchased the book from and type in your review.

With that said, here's Guitar Head signing off!

Until next time then? I'll see you in another book.

THE END

Made in the USA
Middletown, DE
16 October 2023

40928153R00091